T0208848

ABRAHAM OF UR

ABRAHAM OF UR

A CRITICAL ANALYSIS OF THE LIFE AND TIMES OF THE PATRIARCH

DAVID A. SNYDER

ABRAHAM OF UR
A CRITICAL ANALYSIS OF THE LIFE AND TIMES OF THE PATRIARCH

iUniverse books may be ordered through booksellers or by contacting:

iUniverse
1663 Liberty Drive
Bloomington, IN 47403
www.iuniverse.com
1-800-Authors (1-800-288-4677)

Because of the dynamic nature of the Internet, any web addresses or links contained in this book may have changed since publication and may no longer be valid. The views expressed in this work are solely those of the author and do not necessarily reflect the views of the publisher, and the publisher hereby disclaims any responsibility for them.

Any people depicted in stock imagery provided by Thinkstock are models, and such images are being used for illustrative purposes only.
Certain stock imagery © Thinkstock.

ISBN: 978-1-4917-7725-1 (sc)
ISBN: 978-1-4917-7726-8 (e)

Library of Congress Control Number: 2015915779

Print information available on the last page.

iUniverse rev. date: 10/27/2015

TABLE OF CONTENTS

To Whom it was that asked me to write this book.

The Lord said to Abram: "Go forth from the land of your relatives and from your father's house to a land that I will show you." (Gen 12: 1)[1]

PREFACE

Therefore the Lord himself will give you this sign; the virgin shall be with child, and bear a son, and you shall name him Immanuel.[2]

Two thousand years ago, the greatest event in the history of mankind occurred. The God that created the universe became a human being. The Incarnation was so important to mankind that the world's current calendar is hinged on time before the birth of Jesus the Christ (B.C)[3] and the time thereafter (A.D.) This event did not happen in a vacuum. God, in His plan for man to know Him, prepared us for this divine appearance. Because of the immensity of the Incarnation, God gave mankind thousands of years to develop an understanding of deity to the point where we could conceive of, and understand, a single transcendent omnipotent God who

---

[2] Isaiah 7:14 Above is from the 1970 version of the NAB Bible. I use it as it best poetically introduces the incarnation. The current version of Isaiah 7:14 from the NABRE is as follows: "Therefore the Lord himself will give you a sign; the young woman, pregnant and about to bear a son, shall name him Emmanuel." *The Septuagint translated the Hebrew term as parthenos, which normally does mean virgin, and this translation underlies Mt 1:23. Emmanuel: the name means "with us is God." Since for the Christian the incarnation is the ultimate expression of God's willingness to "be with us," it is understandable that this text was interpreted to refer to the birth of Christ.* (NABRE, Footnotes)

[3] B.C. = Before Christ- Today it is more politically correct to use the terms B.C.E. (Before the Common Era). A.D. = Anno Domini which means *In the year of our Lord*. The secular term is C.E. (Common Era) we will us AD and BC in this work.

created all there is – the concept of monotheism that led to the Christianity that we practice today. This work will study that development.

The essence of this book is to give the reader a fuller understanding of the world in which Abraham of Ur lived when he received the word of God four thousand years ago. For this reason we will review the ancient history of where Abraham lived before during and after he left his homeland for the land of Canaan. We will also discover how secular history influenced and helped form our understanding of monotheism practiced in Judaism, Christianity and Islam today. The desire of man to know God has been a long journey. This study will show that at first man created his gods in man's own image. Only later, with the help of the Holy Spirit, will the authors of the Hebrew Scriptures teach us that God created man in His image. We will study the history of the time that the Hebrew patriarchs first received the word from God that they were to be His chosen people. Most importantly, we will discover that *Evolution* and *Revelation* are not mutually exclusive -- they can and did develop side by side.

Most books that consider these subjects look primarily to the development of a theology and do not consider in detail how the civilization and culture of the time affected these doctrinal developments. We will discover and digest some of the theological practices of ancient Mesopotamia and Canaan. Not being ordained or trained in theology, I will not try to justify or admonish these practices; but, one does not need to be trained in theology to compare history and science to Holy Scripture to help us better understand our religion.

Abraham's role in God's Plan

In His chosen time, God will direct a Semitic man named Abram from the ancient city of Ur in southern Mesopotamia to lead his clan to the land of Canaan. From there God will slowly reveal to Abram and his descendants that He is their God and that there is no other. This will be a strange revelation to this man Abram, as all of humanity at this time in history worshiped a pantheon of gods. We will follow the life of this Abram whom God will later name Abraham. We will discover that he may have been as great a secular figure as he was a Biblical one. At the same time, we may be disappointed to discover that while Abraham is called the father of monotheism, the monotheism that he practiced was probably far from the one we claim today.

As we study the Hebrew Scriptures, we will see that the secular world was reluctant to release its theology of polytheism. God's prophets, called by the Holy Spirit time and again over fifteen hundred years, will wage a long war with the world around them until finally Abraham's people will be ready to accept the *anointed one of God* -- the *Messiah* -- the *Christ* that the prophets constantly foretold would come. Only after Abraham's clan, later known as the Jews, were able to accept *the God of Abraham* as the only God was man ready to accept God in the form of his humanity.

At first I was not sure that Abraham even existed. After I investigated the secular history of the day and considered the Ugaritic literature, the Hyksos and the Tell el-Amarna tablets that we will detail later, I came to realize that the geopolitical climate at the time Abraham entered Canaan was perfectly conducive to support the stories of his travels into *the Promised Land*. I will attempt to show the reader that as a slave-owning citizen of the Third Dynasty of Ur in 2000 BC, Abraham's family was well-educated, literate and wealthy. And if we are to believe Josephus, Abraham was possibly an astronomer and military leader. This is contradictory to the image most people have of Abraham as a nomadic shepherd leading a flock of sheep; however, I believe that only a well-educated and worldly man such as Abraham would be able to achieve the goal that God gave to him – to establish the Hebrew nation.

A Challenge to Our Faith

The primary focus of this work is history, not theology. If, like me, the reader becomes more aware of the highly advanced and exciting time in human history that Abraham lived, then I will have accomplished the purpose of the book. This being said, the reader may be surprised and at first even threatened by some of the similarities of stories that we will study of ancient Sumer and Akkad with those found in the first five books of the Bible. Our first thought may be that perhaps the Hebrew Scriptures are not the word of God but plagiarized from men in a pagan society. But, as we develop the story of man's search for God, we will find that the ancient concept of deity was man's first attempt at trying to understand the mystical world around him and was but a stepping stone to the final concept of God that all monotheistic religions now share. By exploring these similarities, we do not want to tarnish the lessons the Holy Spirit has revealed in the Hebrew Scriptures, but rather to augment their historicity and give greater credence to some of the stories.

Most references in this study will be referred to as the Hebrew Scriptures rather than the Old Testament. This description is in respect to my Orthodox Jewish friends and to the fact that during the development of monotheism we are not primarily looking at these stories from a Christian perspective, but from the perspective of our elder brethren, the Jews, who gave this theology to us. As we will be going back and forth in time when studying the life of Abraham, we will use the name Abraham over Abram in most cases.

INTRODUCTION

A CRITICAL EXAMINATION
OF SCRIPTURE

In order to discover the sacred authors' intentions, the reader must take into account the conditions of their times and culture, the literary genres in use at the time, and the modes of feeling, speaking, and narrating then current.[4]

The purpose of this book is to apply the admonition above to the study of the patriarch Abraham, the son of Terah, as found in the book of Genesis in the Hebrew Scriptures. As we will see, there have been an abundance of discoveries by Biblical scholars in recent years that will help us in this endeavor. Most of the discoveries of secular history of the Middle East that concern the study of the Hebrew Scriptures occurred over the last two hundred and fifty years. These discoveries led Bible scholars and theologians to examine Scripture in an entirely new light. There has been ample evidence that the Hebrew Scriptures may well have been influenced by ancient stories in pagan societies. This brought about a new form of

---

[4] Rev. Peter M.J. Stravinskas, Catechism of the Catholic Church, ed. (Hereafter CCC), (Ignatius Press, English translation, 1994), Article III, Sacred Scripture, Para. 110

scripture study which came to be known as the *Historical-Critical Method*[5]. This meant that secular history was now to be considered in interpreting the scriptures and not faith alone. Notwithstanding the quick spread of this form of study, the Historical-Critical method of Bible study had its share of serious criticism as many non-religious secular scholars have tried to use this approach to disprove the influence of God in the Scriptures. The proper use of this method is to let our secular discoveries augment our faith in the Hebrew Scriptures rather than taint our beliefs that the works are inspired by the Holy Spirit. This is difficult for those who profess a literal translation of Scripture. Many Protestant theologians, as a result of the Reformation, had forsaken the Roman Catholic Church's theology of truth through *Scripture and Tradition* for that of *Sola Scriptura* (scripture alone). As a result Scripture, their primary base of faith, was being threatened. Still, most of the leading scholars who used this method were Protestant Bible scholars from England and Germany, and it was later used in the United States. Many of these theologians led the academic world in the translation of these new discoveries in a quest to understand more fully the *genesis of Genesis*.

The Catholic Church and Historical Criticism

Up until the time of the Second Vatican Council in 1962, the Catholic Church had not paid much attention to this new method of study. After all, the Church still had its *Tradition*[6]. A challenge to the historical correctness of Scripture did not threaten its core beliefs; however, some of this study was so persuasive that the Church, although some would say late coming to this study, recognized that it must inform the faithful of its position on these new revelations. Pope Pius XII in his Encyclical on

---

5   Historical Critical Method, AKA Historical Criticism or Higher Criticism is a branch of literary criticism that investigates the origins of ancient text in order to understand *the world behind the text*. Soulen, Richard N.; Soulen, R. Kendall (2001). Handbook of biblical criticism (3rd ed., rev. and expanded.) Louisville, Ky. Westminster John Knox Press, pg. 78.

6   The theological term *Tradition* comes from the Latin meaning "handing over." In the religious sense, it is the teaching and practices handed down, whether it is oral or in written form, separately from but not independently of Scripture. (Catholic Encyclopedia,(1998, Our Sunday Visitor Publishing Division) Pg. 971

promoting Biblical Studies, ***Divino Afflante Spiritu***[7] when commenting on historical criticism said:

> 13. *We also, by this Encyclical Letter, desire to insure that the work may not only proceed without interruption, but may also daily become more perfect and fruitful; and to that end We are specially intent on pointing out to all what yet remains to be done, with what spirit the Catholic exegete should undertake, at the present day, so great and noble a work, and to give new incentive and fresh courage to the laborers who toil so strenuously in the vineyard of the Lord.*

One of the sixteen documents of Vatican II, DEI VERBUM[8], was written on the subject of sacred scripture, and some of it deals with this new exegesis. It first advises that what Scripture tells us is what God wishes us to know. The document states in part:

> "Since, therefore, all that the inspired authors, or sacred writers, affirm should be regarded as affirmed by the Holy Spirit, we must acknowledge that the books of Scripture, firmly, faithfully and without error, teach that truth which God, for the sake of our salvation, wished to see confided to the sacred scriptures."[9]

Notwithstanding the secular history we will discover in this study, I firmly agree with this statement. The canon of Sacred Scriptures that we recognize as the Bible today was inspired by the Holy Spirit, regardless of where the authors obtained the information transferred therein. DEI VERBUM and the Catechism of the Catholic Church under *The senses of*

---

[7] Encyclical of Pope Pius XII on promoting Biblical Studies, Commemorating the Fifteenth anniversary of Providentissimus Deus, Sep. 30, 1945.

[8] Dogmatic Constitution on Divine Revelations, 18 November, 1965, Flannery, Austin, OP, Ed. "The Basic Sixteen Documents, Vatican II Constitutions, Decrees, Declarations" ed., (Costello Publishing Co. Inc.,1996) Pg. 97

[9] Ibid, Chapter III, Par. 11, pg. 105

Scripture[10] teaches that the faithful should distinguish between two senses of Scripture, the literal and the spiritual – the latter being subdivided into the *allegorical, moral, and anagogical senses*[11]. Considering the sense of scripture in another way, the Church is saying that the faithful is not required to accept the entire Hebrew Scriptures as factual history.

In this book we will frequently refer to scientific discoveries that concern the history of the Hebrews and particularly stories in the book of Genesis, which brings up the issue of science and scripture. I am well aware that some of the theories of this work will be controversial and threatening to some of the faithful. To address this concern, I have again found the answer in the Catechism of the Catholic Church. It tells us that whatever we discover in nature, we must always relate our knowledge to the glory of God:

> "The question about the origins of the world and of man has been the object of many scientific studies which have splendidly enriched our knowledge of the age and dimensions of the cosmos, the development of life-forms and the appearance of man. These discoveries invite us to even greater admiration for the greatness of the Creator ... The great interest accorded to these studies is strongly stimulated by a question of another order, which goes beyond the proper domain of the natural sciences. It is not only a question of knowing when and how the universe arose physically, or when man appeared, but rather of discovering the meaning of such an origin: is the universe governed by chance, blind fate, anonymous necessity, or by a transcendent, intelligent and good Being called God"?[12]

Finally, we are fortunate that Pope Emeritus Benedict the XVI has recently given us his opinion on the Historical-Critical Method in his book *Light of*

---

[10]   CCC, Paragraph 115-119, pg. 33

[11]   Ibid, 115, pg. 33

[12]   Ibid, 283-284, pg. 74

the World¹³. This section begins with a question from Peter Seewald, who articulates many of the concerns of this method which is still held within some parts of the Vatican.

> SEEWALD: *The historical-critical method had its merits, but it also led fatefully to an erroneous development. Its attempt to demythologize the Bible produced a terrible superficiality and blindness toward the deeper layers and profound message of Scripture. What is more, looking back, we realize that the alleged facts cited for the last two hundred years by the skeptic's intent on relativizing pretty much every statement of the Bible were in many cases nothing more than mere hypotheses. Shouldn't we be much clearer than we have been that the exegetes have to some extent been practicing a pseudo-science whose operative principle is not Christian, but an anti-Christian animus, and that it has led millions of people astray?*

> POPE EMERITUS BENEDICT: *I wouldn't subscribe to so harsh a judgment. The application of the historical method to the Bible as a historical text was a path that had to be taken. If we believe that Christ is real history, and not myth, then the testimony concerning him has to be historically accessible as well. In this sense, the historical method has also given us many gifts. It has brought us back closer to the text and its originality; it has shown us more precisely how it grew, and much more besides. The historical-critical method will always remain one dimension of interpretation. Vatican II made this clear. On the one hand, it presents the essential elements of the historical method as a necessary part of access to the Bible. At the same time, though, it adds that the Bible has to be read in the same Spirit in which it was written.*

---

¹³ *Light of the World: The Pope, The Church and the signs of the times*, Peter Seewald, Pope Benedict XVI, Ignatius Press, San Francisco, 2010

It has to be read in its wholeness, in its unity. And that can be done only when we approach it as a book of the People of God progressively advancing toward Christ. What is needed is not simply a break with the historical method, but a self-critique of the historical method; a self-critique of historical reason that takes cognizance of its limits and recognizes the compatibility of a type of knowledge that derives from faith; in short, we need a synthesis between an exegesis that operates with historical reason and an exegesis that is guided by faith. We have to bring the two things into a proper relationship to each other. That is also a requirement of the basic relationship between faith and reason.

It seems the retired Pope is saying that all future study of Scripture by the Catholic Church will consider the Historical-Critical Method of study to some degree with some reservations how it should be studied. It is quite interesting that some secular scholars using the Historical-Critical Method, rather than proving that Scripture is a fable or worthless stories, end up substantiating or even proving stories within Scripture. It is as if our God, with a very good sense of humor, is letting the unbelieving secular world find out for itself what we the faithful have known from the beginning – the Scriptures are the Truth that God wants us to know.

Who Wrote the Bible?

With the Historical-Critical Method of Bible study firmly in place in the minds of most Biblical scholars, the next great challenge was to analyze just who wrote the Hebrew Scriptures and when they were reduced to the form that we read today. As the Historical-Critical Method of study increased, Biblical scholars as far back as the 17th century began to look for ways to reconcile the inconsistencies in scripture. They identified up to four different sources of input into the first five books of the Bible – the Torah. Since that time, there has been a persuasive argument known by Biblical scholars as the *Documentary Hypothesis* or *Four Source theory*[14]. This theory tries to explain the "doublets" and "triplets" of stories within the Hebrew Scripture, such as the different creation and flood stories that are placed right after each other and are sometimes contradictory. Many of these stories are clearly written in different styles, grammar and from differing religious and political perspectives. Based on this theory, it is possible to conclude that each author wrote the same stories from the perspective of his own time and place. A German Biblical scholar, Julius Wellhausen, was one of the first to identify and classify these four sources as follows:

1. The "J" or Yahwistic source (Yahweh in German) written about 950 BC in the southern kingdom of Judah. It refers to God throughout as Yahweh and the kingdom of Judah is paramount.
2. The "E" Elohist source written about 850 BC in the northern kingdom of Israel probably by a Levite priest. It refers to God as El or Elohim throughout and de- emphasizes the kingdom of Judah.
3. The "D" Deuteronomist source written about 600 BC in Jerusalem during the period of religious reform. It emphasizes the history of Israel from a perspective of king Josiah of Judah.
4. The "P" Priestly source written about 500 BC by Jewish priests in exile in Babylon. It emphasizes temple worship in one location in Jerusalem as proclaimed by King Hezekiah.

Finally someone, called a redactor, put all four of these sources into one work, the Hebrew Scripture that we have today. It would be the same as if someone took all four of the New Testament Gospels and put them into one book – but keeping the original words of each author. If this hypothesis is true, the final redactor must have been a literary genius to be able to capture all of the versions and make it look like one work – a work that is the most read book in the history of man.

---

[14] The *documentary hypothesis*, (DH) (sometimes called the *Wellhausen hypothesis*), proposes that the Pentateuch (the first five books of the Bible) was derived from originally independent, parallel and complete narratives, which were subsequently combined into the current form by a series of redactors (editors). Wikipedia

Richard Friedman in his book *Who wrote the Bible,*[15] and his follow-up book, *The Bible with sources Revealed,*[16] gives a detailed analysis as to why each separate author was inclined to write as he did. When one looks at the conflicting styles and perspectives side by side as Friedman does in his works, it is quite clear that this hypothesis has great credibility. *The Four Source Theory* is so well understood in today's Biblical studies that many authors will simply refer to the "P" or "E" source without explaining the theory itself. Friedman's timeline is somewhat different from Wellhausen by positing that the Hebrew Scripture that has come down to us was written in the court of King Hezekiah between 722 and 609 BC, possibly by the author of the book of Jeremiah.

This theory complicates the accepted Hebrew tradition that Moses was the author of the first five books of the Bible. This is an anathema to Orthodox Jews and many Evangelical Christians, who interpret the Bible literally. In my opinion, even if the Documentary Hypothesis is correct, one can easily accept that Moses was the original author of these oral traditions revealed by Yahweh. The four sources clearly wrote their individual story from one core source. Many studies of oral tradition show that an original story changes considerably as time passes. It is more important to us today to focus on the fact that the theological lessons espoused by Moses were given to him by the Holy Spirit on Mount Sinai. As we shall develop in detail in this work, however, there is a serious question as to where Moses received the information that he relates in the Torah.

The Chronology of the Bible

While it is difficult to determine with any certainty the dates the patriarchs come and go in history, Jewish tradition does give us some help. The *Seder Olam Rabbah* which means, *the great order of the world,* was written in second century AD by the rabbis writing the Jerusalem Talmud. It is considered the doctrinal text for historical understanding of Jewish

---

[15] Richard Elliot Friedman, *Who Wrote the Bible?"* (New York: Harper and Row, Publishers, 1987)

[16] Ibid, *The Bible with Sources Revealed, A new view into the five books of Moses"* (New York: Harper Collins Publishers, 2003)

Talmudic tradition.[17] It lists the chronology of Biblical dates taken literally from the books of the Torah and gives the equivalent secular date in BC and AD. For instance, it states that Abraham was born 1948 years after creation, which was the year 1976 BC. We will use the dates in the Seder Olam in this study for the early patriarchs even though their lifespans stretch our credibility more than those starting with Abraham, Isaac and Jacob. We should also keep in mind that the life expectancy at this time in history was extremely low compared to today due to infant mortality rates.[18] In my opinion the Hebrew Scripture disparity with the life expectancy of humans as known by science today is more damaging to the credibility of the Bible than any of the stories. The was memorialized in the infamous *Scopes monkey trial*[19] where Clarence Darrow, a well-known civil rights lawyer, defended John Scopes who was put on trial by the state of Tennessee for teaching *Evolution*. In the trial Darrow put Scope's defense attorney, William Jennings Bryan, a three time Presidential candidate and an evangelical minister on the stand. When Bryan tried to defend the ages of the patriarchs in Genesis, Darrow destroyed his and Scriptures credibility which gave the secular press of 1925 great ammunition in their war against the divine inspiration of Scripture. The Jewish *Book of Jubilees* states that all generations after Abraham will have what we would consider normal life expectancies of one and half Jubilees with a Jubilee being 49 years.[20] My personal theory is that most ages stated in Genesis for Abraham are about twice the normal age.

The chronology of the Bible is not an exact science. There are three basic sets of dates used by Biblical Scholars: the Hebrew dates in the

---

[17] See: "*Seder Olam: The Rabbinic View of Biblical Chronology*", Heinrich W. Guggenheimer, Ed. (Maryland: Rowman and Littlefield Publishers, Inc., 1998)

[18] Encyclopaedia Britannica in 1961 estimated the life expectancy at birth in the Bronze and Iron Age at 26. In classical Rome if the child lasted until age 10, the life expectancy increased an additional 35 to 37 years (total age 45 to 47)

[19] There was a movie of this trial with the title: **Inherit the Wind** is a 1960 Hollywood film adaptation of the play of the same name, written by Jerome Lawrence and Robert Edwin Lee, directed by Stanley Kramer.

[20] Jub. 23: 8-15, First found at Qumran. It is like Genesis except it rehashes history into 49 year segments called Jubilees (*Life after Death*, Segal, and pg. 353).

Seder Olam and Masoretic Texts, the Samaritan dates[21] and the dates in the Septuagint translation of the Hebrew Scriptures.[22] Below is a chart showing an example of the chronology of the Bible.[23] AM dates mean *"Dates from Creation."*

EVENT	YEAR AM	YEAR BC	SPAN
Creation to Adam	0	3924 BC	
Birth of Abraham (Gen 11:26)	1948	1976 BC	1948
Promise to Abraham	2018	1906 BC	70
Birth of Isaac	2048	1876 BC	30
Descent into Egypt by Joseph	2238	1686 BC	190
Exodus from Egypt (Ex 12:40)	2448	1476 BC	210[24]

The Canon of the Bible

Christians refer to the Bible as Sacred Scripture and the word of God. The Bible, which included Hebrew Scriptures and the New Testament, was written by men inspired by the Holy Spirit; not dictated to man from God as is the belief of Moslems about the Qur'an. For that reason it is not perfect history or consistent throughout. The original Hebrew Scriptures were in the Hebrew language until after the Babylonian exile in 580 BC, where the common language of the Jews became Aramaic. Most of the Scriptures were then written in the Aramaic language until Alexander the Great controlled the Middle East, and Greek became the language of intellectual discourse. The Scriptures were then translated into Greek and became known as the Septuagint or LXX (the Roman word and numeral for 70). This nomenclature was given to represent the 72 rabbis who read the translation from Aramaic and Hebrew into Greek and said it was perfect. This was the Hebrew Scriptures that Our Lord read when

---

[21] Samaritans: The remnants of the Northern Kingdom of Israel. They claim direct descent from Moses and have a slightly different translation of the Torah from the Jews of Judea. A few of them still exist in the West Bank area of Israel; and they still practice a temple sacrifice.

[22] Septuagint: A translation of the Hebrew Scriptures into Greek.

[23] Chronology of the Bible, Wikipedia.

[24] 430 years from promise to Abraham; 400 from birth of Isaac.

He spoke in the Synagogues. The Septuagint included several books such as II Maccabees; Wisdom and Daniel 13, 14 in the original Greek and some original Aramaic books which only survived in Greek such as Judith, Baruch, Sirach and I Maccabees. In 90 AD, the canon of the Hebrew Scriptures was revised by the rabbinic school at Jamnia[25], which chose to eliminate the books written in Greek listed above. One would think that after being dominated by the Greeks and then the Romans, the Jews decided they had had enough of foreign influence in their Scriptures.

The Septuagint was translated by St. Jerome at the request of Pope Damasus I in 382 AD into Latin, which came to be known as the Vulgate. This version of both the Hebrew Scriptures and the New Testament became the Bible used by all of Christianity until the time of the Protestant Reformation in the 15th century. At that time the reformers chose to accept only the Hebrew Scriptural canon accepted by the Janine school of Judaism, thus eliminating the several books mentioned above. The Protestants today call these missing books *Apocryphal Scriptures*. Catholics refer to them as deuterocanonical.

The canon[26] of the Roman and Eastern Catholic Churches seem to have been first presented at the Council of Hippo in northern Africa in 393 AD, which was under the authority of the local bishop, St. Augustine. The findings of this council are not extant but were read and accepted by the subsequent Councils of Carthage in 397 and 419 AD which are available. Pope Damasus I held a council in Rome in 382 AD, where he issued a Biblical canon identical to the ones at Hippo and Carthage. For a while some of the Eastern Churches had a problem with the book of Revelation;

---

[25] Heinrick Graetz proposed the theory of the Jamnia Council in 1871. His theory survived through most of the twentieth century. Some scholars now refute the existence of the council.

[26] "The word *canon* as applied to the Scriptures has long had a special and consecrated meaning. In its fullest comprehension it signifies the authoritative list or closed number of the writings composed under Divine inspiration, and destined for the well-being of the Church, using the latter word in the wide sense of the theocratic society which began with God's revelation of Himself to the people of Israel." Catholic Encyclopedia. "It was by the apostolic Tradition that the Church discerned which writings were to be included in the list of the sacred books; this complete list is called the *canon of Scripture*". CCC120

however, by the fifth century this was rectified and from that time forward there has been unanimous acceptance of this canon in the Roman and Eastern Catholic Churches.[27]

Hebrew Tradition

Just as Scripture and tradition are the bases of Roman Catholic theology, so did the Hebrew people in addition to Scripture also rely on an oral and written tradition that they called the Talmud. The Talmud is written in Hebrew and Aramaic and consists of 63 tractates on over 6200 pages. It contains the thoughts of thousands of rabbis over the years on subjects as varied as law, ethics, philosophy, customs, and theology, and to our interest, history. It is not dogma however as are some traditions in the Catholic Church. Originally, the sages and teachers of the *Law* passed on their interpretations of the *Book* to each generation in schools of Hebrew theology just as when St. Paul was **educated at the feet of the great teacher Gamaliel**[28]

Shortly after the fall of the northern kingdom of Israel, Jerusalem too was conquered by the Babylonians, who took its people captive back to Babylon until they were allowed to return in full by Cyrus the Great of Persia some seventy years later. During the Jews' captivity in Babylon, the religious leaders realized that to keep the God of Abraham, Isaac and Jacob alive in the minds of the people, they must write down the traditions of their religion as well as maintain the *Book*.[29] Thus the Babylonian Talmud was written.

After the destruction of the Temple in Jerusalem by the Romans in 70 AD, Judaism as a sacrificial religion ceased to exist. Judaism from that time on will be a rabbinical religion as it is today. To maintain the written and unwritten law for future centuries (until the temple could be rebuilt), the rabbis of the early Christian era, therefore, wrote the Jerusalem Talmud.

---

[27] Catholic Encyclopedia, Bible, pg. 142-143

[28] Act. 22: 3

[29] The Book: Another word for Hebrew Scriptures. Mohammad will use the same word for the Hebrew Scriptures in the Qur'an.

Another source of Hebrew Tradition is the *Masoretic Text,*[30] which is the reproduction, but not interpretation, of the Hebrew Scriptures by Jewish Bible scholars known as the Masoretes. They collected all known sources of the Hebrew Scriptures in the 6th through the 10th centuries AD in Babylon and Palestine. As original Hebrew did not include vowels, the Masoretes added vowel signs to make for clearer pronunciations for future readers. The study from the city of Tiberius in Galilee eventually became the standard and is frequently quoted by Biblical scholars as the source of tradition in the Jewish Faith.[31] As we shall see in Chapter 9, The Gods of Canaan, these Masoretes, who were living in a post-Christian world, also changed a word or two in the Hebrew Scriptures to avoid embarrassing passages that refer to the coming Messiah.

The Historian Flavius Josephus

In this narrative, we will frequently refer to the Jewish historian Flavius Josephus' work *The Antiquities of the Jews*[32] which was written for the Romans after the fall of Jerusalem. Josephus was a Pharisee of noble priestly heritage. While Josephus is a great historian, he was also a very interesting character in Jewish history. Many Jews look on Josephus as a traitor claiming he assisted the Romans during their conquest of Jerusalem when the Temple was destroyed in 70 AD.[33] Nonetheless, Josephus was a Jewish patriot, who was appointed by King Agrippa and approved by the Sanhedrin in Jerusalem as governor and general of Galilee during the Roman occupation. In his autobiography, Josephus tells his side of the story claiming he maintained order in Galilee to prevent civil war of

---

[30] Masoretic Text: from Hebrew masoreth, "tradition", traditional Hebrew text of the Jewish Bible, meticulously assembled and codified, and supplied with diacritical marks to enable correct pronunciation. (Encyclopaedia Britannica)

[31] Ibid, http://www.britannica.com/EBchecked/topic/368081/Masoretic-text

[32] *Josephus, The Complete Works,* William Whiston, A.M, ed. (Nashville: Thomas Nelson Publisher, 1998), pg. 30

[33] Josephus claims he assisted the Romans by pleading with his fellow Jews to lay down their arms to avoid certain destruction of hundreds of thousands of his fellow Jews. He became friends with Titus who allowed him to preserve the "holy books" in the Temple prior to it's' destruction. Titus took Josephus to Rome, made him a Roman citizen and gave him considerable land and wealth.

the many factions so that they could remain united in their war with the Romans. Josephus himself led an army against the Romans, was captured when his horse fell in a quagmire and imprisoned by the Romans. He maintained a friendship with most of the Roman leaders after the war and wrote *Antiquities* for the library in Rome. This was about a hundred years before the Jerusalem Talmud was written. Therefore, we can assume that Josephus obtained his knowledge of ancient Hebrew culture from the Hebrew Scriptures and the Babylonian Talmud. Notwithstanding his questioned loyalty to the Jews, Josephus is a credible source of Hebrew tradition.

Extra-Biblical Discoveries

Before we begin to discover the culture that Abraham lived in Mesopotamia and Canaan in the following chapters, it is important to understand some of the extra-Biblical evidence in secular history that we will see frequently in our study of Abraham. The science of archaeology and linguistic studies has increased exponentially over the last two hundred years so much so that new discoveries are made almost every day that gives us a better knowledge of the culture, literature and history of the ancient Near East. Some of these discoveries are making us reanalyze how our understanding of deity has come to be. Satellite imagery has given us a new way to look at our planet, and we now see things that we could not discern from landlocked perspectives. This has given us the chance to see ancient rivers mentioned in Scripture that seemed to have disappeared, to locate abandoned cities that have been covered with time, to discover that deserts were at one time lush environments, and that oceans and continents were once other than they are today. The recent explosion of climate change studies using glacial stratification and sediment core samples has given geologists a clearer picture of the time line of century long droughts and ice ages that have come and gone during man's evolution, giving us a better idea of when and where man developed civilized society. Every year new discoveries are pushing back the age of man's civilization by thousands of years. This information and data, which scientists have been able to translate over the years through the evolution of technology, provides a new perspective on history and man's development that is not similarly developed in the Hebrew Scriptures.

After the fall of the Ottoman Empire after World War I, the colonial powers of Europe divided the Middle East into areas of influence. France was given the newly created countries of Syria and Lebanon while England was given Iraq and Egypt. Due to the influence of Islam in this area since the sixth century AD, there had been little or no interest in ancient civilizations in the Middle East; therefore, remnants of ancient civilizations sat untouched for centuries. Because of the advanced schools of scientific inquiry in the European countries, whenever some local inhabitant found some old thing in a field or in a cave, he would notify the colonial authorities, who would then bring in experts from Europe. If the finds were of interest, the museums of these countries sponsored archeological expeditions that made some incredible discoveries about this area of the world – especially for those interested in Biblical studies. Some of the artifacts that they discovered are described here.

Steles, Ostraca, Seals and Scarabs

A *stele* is an upright stone or slab with an inscribed or sculptured surface, used as a monument or as a commemorative tablet in or on the face of a building. They were usually made to tell of the greatness or victories of a king or ruler. In 1868 a stele, called the *Moabite Stone*, also called *the Mesha Stele,* was discovered in the state of Jordan in 1868 by F. A. Klein[34], in what was the territory of Moab in around 930 BC. It is an incredible secular find giving extra-Biblical proof of the historical king of Israel Omni and his son Ahab as found in the book of II Kings:

> **Now Mesha, king of Moab, who raised sheep, used to pay the king of Israel a tribute of a hundred thousand lambs and wool of a hundred thousand lambs. But when Ahab died, the king of Moab had rebelled against the King of Israel.[35]**

---

[34] Frederick Augustus Klein (1827–1903), or F. A. Klein as he is called in much of the literature, was a Church Missionary Society (CMS) missionary in the Middle East. He is remembered for his 1868 discovery of the Moabite Stone, which dates from about 840 B.C. (Wikipedia)

[35] II Kings 3:4-5

The number of sheep and lambs may be exaggerated and much of scripture and ancient steles do just that because they are usually written by the victor. The Moabite Stone tells a similar story:

> "I Mesha ... King of Moab, reined over Moab thirty years. As for Omni, king of Israel, he humbled Moab many years. ... Now Omni had occupied the land of Medeba, and Israel had dwelt there in his time and half the time of his son Ahab."

> "Now the men of Gad had always dwelt in the land of Ataroth, and the king of Israel had built Ataroth for them";[36]

This second quote from the stele confirms the presence of the Transjordan Tribes of Israel that Moses allowed to stay in the land of Moab as we see below:

> *Joshua addressed the Reubenites, the Gadites, and the half-tribe of Manasseh: "Remember what Moses, the servant of the Lord, commanded you when he said, 'The Lord, your God, is about to give you rest; he will give you this land.'"[37]*

Other Palestinian inscriptions have been found over the years that not only confirm historical figures in Scripture but also enhance our knowledge of the ancient Hebrew language by giving scholars a better understanding of the grammar and style of letters used in times past.

Ostraca are potsherds or parts of pottery found in archeological digs. Many were just broken pottery adorned with scriptural verses written on fire hardened pottery. When its use was finished, the pottery was thrown into a dump of similar potsherds to be found by archeologists today, which

---

[36] *"Ancient Near Eastern Texts, Relating to the Old Testament"*, James B. Pritchard, ed. (New Jersey: Princeton University Press, 3rd Edition with Supplement, 1969), pg. 320 (hereafter Pritchard)

[37] Jos 1:12-13

cherish the tremendous knowledge that they display. An archeologist who knows the depth and location of the potsherds within the site can give a reasonable time frame of the contents. Carbon dating gives an even greater basis for dating such finds. Many times the commercial transaction of the contents of the pottery itself was listed as in the case of the *Samarian Ostraca,* which scholars believe were written during the reign of Jeroboam II in about 778-780 BC. The Lachish Ostraca found in 1935, relate stories of the Chaldean siege of Lachish in the year 589 or 588 BC, which was the time of Jeremiah and confirms some of his writings. Also of interest is the discovery of the *Siloam Inscription,* which was found in the lower entrance to the tunnel of Hezekiah south of the temple area in Jerusalem. It tells of the actual construction of the tunnel including the final connection of the two work crews coming together at the center of the tunnel.[38] And, of course, the Dead Sea Scrolls, which are among the oldest extant records of the Hebrew Scriptures, substantiate the correct translation from Hebrew into Greek of the Septuagint version of the Old Testament that we read today.

Circular seals were also found in great numbers throughout Mesopotamia. They were intricately carved to tell an ancient tale or epic story. When the seals were rolled onto soft clay they identified the owner of the seal who used it as a signature for commerce and legal matters. They are of interest to historians as they are sometime the only record of certain events in history.

Scarabs were carved amulets in ancient Egypt that were many times worn as jewelry and rings. They originally depicted religious or political affiliations but came to be ornamental in later dynasties. These too are helpful to historians as they sometimes give the name of the Pharaoh or his administrator and the dates of his reign. These also were used as seals for commerce.

The Tell el- Amarna Tablets

In 1887, a peasant woman in Egypt was digging in a hill between the ancient ruins of Memphis and Luxor – known today as Tell el-Amarna. While digging she discovered a few ancient small clay tablets ranging

---

[38] Pritchard, Palestinian Inscription, pg. 320-322

from two by two and half inches in size to three by nine inches. When a villager saw that the tablets had some funny writing on them, he figured they may be worth something and notified an American missionary who immediately contacted the Egyptian authorities. What she had found was the royal archives of the Pharaohs Amenhotep III (who changed his name to Akhenatem)[39] and his son Tutankhamum, who ruled Egypt from about 1388 to 1332 BC. The 382 tablets found to date were diplomatic letters to and from the Egyptian king with monarchs, governors and provincial leaders in Babylon, Syria, Mitanni, Canaan and even Crete. They were written in a slightly revised form of cuneiform writing from ancient Akkad probably using the Ugaritic form of cuneiform, which by this time had evolved into an alphabet. Many Biblical scholars consider the information gained from the Tell el-Amarna Tablets (hereafter Amarna Letters) equal to the Dead Sea Scrolls because the information provided in the letters has provided substantial insight into the Canaanite civilization at or near the time of the patriarchs. They also provide an extra-Biblical source confirming stories of the Hebrews in Canaan shortly after the Exodus – particularly the tales disclosed in the books of Exodus and Joshua. More important to historians is the fact that the Amarna Letters give a certain date of 1388 to 1332 B.C to confirm political events at this time in history.

---

[39] Amenhotep III changed his name to Akhenatem as a reverence to the sun-god Atem. Akhenatem is considered by many scholars as the founder of monotheism as he denied all other gods except the sun-god Atem who he claimed created the universe. This theology was an anathema to the priestly class of polytheists in Thebes. This may have been the reason he moved his capital to Amarna which seems to have been abandoned after his death (Archaeology Magazine, May/June, 2014, pg. 24-30). While there is considerable controversy over this claim of him being the first monotheist, it seems clear from existing evidence that he acknowledged other Egyptian gods making his theology henotheism or more likely monolatry -- which we will see in Chapter One was the theology as far back as Abraham's time in Mesopotamia and Canaan. After his death Egypt returned to its pure polytheist religion. (see Wikipedia for Amarna Letters and Akhenatem)

CHAPTER ONE

ABRAHAM THE SON OF TERAH

These are the descendants of Terah. Terah begot
Abram, Nahor and Haran, and Haran begot Lot.
Haran died before Terah his father, in his native
land, in Ur of the Chaldeans.[40]

Moses tells us in Genesis that Terah, the father of Abraham, was a descendant of Eber who was traditionally considered the father of the Hebrews. All were descendants of Noah after the flood. To the Jews, and to Christians who have inherited Jewish traditions, this story is one of the critical points in the narrative of God's Plan of Salvation. Abram, who God will rename Abraham, will from this time forward be known as *Our Father Abraham* by Jews, Christians and Muslims. Monotheism will shortly take its first steps into history.

Is Abraham Just a Legend?

Did this story of Terah and Abraham really happen? Did Abraham even exist? Many Biblical scholars today who use the Historical-Critical method of study argue that because there is no extant written history of Terah or Abraham, this story is more than likely a legend, a fable or an allegory to make a theological point. It is clear that many stories in the Hebrew Scriptures are exaggerated legends such as Jonah and the whale and the

---

[40] Gen 11: 27-28

unbelievable ages of the early patriarchs. This does not mean that all of the stories have no historical value. For instance, Genesis states that *Nimrod* built cities throughout Shinar including Nineveh.[41] Assyrian legends speak of a *Nimbus*, who also built cities including Nineveh making linguists consider Nimbus as Nimrod.[42] We will find many more men of history who are also men of the Bible. Possibly we can use the study of ancient history to confirm with extant data that Abraham was a man of history in ancient Mesopotamia. Sacred Scripture itself can help us understand the secular history at the time of Abraham. For example, Genesis does not tell us that Terah worshiped pagan gods; however, Joshua tells us later:

> *"In times past your ancestors down to Terah, father of Abraham and Nahor, lived beyond the River and served other gods."* [43]

That Terah would serve gods other than Yahweh is quite logical to those who study ancient history as Terah lived in the city-state of Ur during its Third Dynasty (Ur III) in about 2000 BC. However, that Joshua would confirm history by telling his people that before Terah all their ancestors were polytheists is amazing considering the words of Genesis that will come later.

Ur itself was founded in the ancient civilization of Sumer near the *Lower Sea* (The Persian Gulf) more than fifteen hundred years before Terah lived there and had a very long history of polytheistic worship. As we shall see, there is extensive evidence that the citizens of Ur, at this time in history, predominantly worshiped the moon god *Sin*, as known by the Akkadians

---

[41] Gen 10:8-10

[42] Nimrod has a reputation within Hebrew and Moslem tradition, including Josephus, as the antithesis of Abraham, who was righteous while Nimrod was wicked; with Nimrod the polytheist and Abraham the monotheist. The historical Nimrod legend is that he is associated with ancient Erech (Urik) and the builder of the city of Akkad. NAB: Nimrod: Probably Tukulti-Ninurta I (thirteenth century BC), the first Assyrian conqueror of Babylon and a famous city-builder at home.

[43] Jos 24:2 that your ancestors down to Terah served other gods was a major issue in the Qur'an also. Verse 21:058 states Abraham broke Terah's Idols into pieces.

and *Nanna* by the earlier Sumerians. It would be highly unusual if Terah and his family did not worship the moon god, Sin.

Terah himself was most likely an Akkadian Semite as his family names are of Akkadian descent and have a relationship with the moon-god *Sin* which is another substantiation of his pagan worship. Abram is the Akkadian *Abu-ramu* which is of west Semitic origin and means *exalted father*. Sarai, Abraham's wife and half-sister from another marriage of Terah, whom God will later call Sarah, is an epithet of the consort of the moon god Sin of Haran. Milcah, Abraham's sister-in-law, is derived from Malkatu, the consort of the sun god Shamash[44]. The relation of the moon-god of Ur and Haran to Abraham and his family might be troubling to some Bible fundamentalists; however, it might also explain why God changed Abram's name to Abraham and Sarai's name to Sarah.

The Semites of Mesopotamia

As descendants of Shem, the son of Noah, Terah and his family were Semites,[45] a semi-nomadic people who share the same language. Historians do not know for sure from where they came. But we can surmise they came into Mesopotamia over eons from the Arabian Peninsula as a result of a major climatic change when the Sahara Desert changed from a land with flowing rivers and green pastures into the desert that it is today.[46] The Semites did not have a written history before learning the cuneiform

---

[44] The Brown-Driver-Briggs Hebrew and English Lexicon, Edward Robinson, ed. Hendrickson Publishers, 1906

[45] Derived from the Greek word for Shem. The Merriam-Webster' Collegiate Dictionary states the word *Semite* and most uses of the word *Semitic* relate to any people whose native tongue is, or was historically, a member of the associated language family. Semites are Near Eastern people which included Akkadians (Assyrians and Babylonians), Eblaites, Ugarites, Canaanites, Phoenicians (including Carthaginians), Hebrews (Israelites, Judeans and Samaritans), Arameans, Chaldeans, Amorites, Moabites, Edomites, Hyksos and Arabs.

[46] Satellite imagery shows a dry river bed running from the Sahara Desert into the area just north of the Persian Gulf into the mouth of the Euphrates and Tigris rivers. Many Bible scholars think this river may be the Pison River mentioned in Gen 2:10-14

system of writing developed in the city states of ancient Sumer. Most Mesopotamians north and west of Sumer, including the Amorites and Canaanites, whom we will see more of in the story of Abraham, were considered Semites although the Canaanites were called *Western Semites* by the Egyptians.

Mesopotamian Polytheism

The author of Genesis tells us little about mankind from the time of Noah until the time of Terah, the father of Abraham. Most of the information in this part of Genesis is genealogies. It is clear from the history of the Near East, however, that the people at the time of Terah all worshiped a pantheon of gods and had done so for at least three thousand years. The same can be said for ancient Egypt, India, China and the Americas. Even though the author of Genesis relates a linear monotheistic theology from the time of Adam to the time of Terah, when Genesis speaks of Abraham we find that God had not yet introduced even the most simplified form of monotheism. Meanwhile, history clearly shows that the worship of many gods in Mesopotamia would have been the norm.

Polytheism itself will change over the centuries from a worship of many gods revealed in mythic epics and stories to a religion more closely related to the monotheism of early Judaism. But this will take a long time, and we are interested in the world of 2000 BC when Terah moved his family from Ur to Haran. We shall also see that the people of Abraham's time were highly educated in mathematics and science – both of which require man's reasoning ability to advance. Therefore, it is understandable that Mesopotamian polytheism would also evolve through reason into a belief in one supreme (although not yet transcendent) god within the pantheon. To put this in perspective, Judaism, Christianity and Islam all developed dogmas and theologies over a similar period of time, but none of these religions are now what they once were. God's revelations to the man Abraham will be a major factor in the evolution of polytheism but not conclusive as we will see from the practice of polytheism by Abraham's descendants in later chapters. The reader may be surprised to find that the polytheism of Abraham's time is still alive in our world today as 21% of the world's population still practices Hinduism and Buddhism which are quite similar to the polytheism of Abraham's time.[47] If we look at the spirituality of Hinduism today, we may have an idea of what the polytheism of Abraham's time would be like today.

Perhaps the greatest discoveries that concern our understanding of how ancient polytheistic religions affected the development of monotheism have been made over the last two hundred and fifty years in an area of the Middle East that the Greeks called *Mesopotamia*. This fertile area bears the illustrious title which means *the land between the rivers*. The two great rivers are the Tigris and Euphrates, which run south out of the Anatolia Mountains in what is now southern Turkey through today's Syria and Iraq into the Persian Gulf. Ancient Mesopotamia is separated into two parts. The northern or fertile section is located from the *Great Sea* (Mediterranean) south to an area near Bagdad in Iraq of today. The southern section of Mesopotamia is the flat land river delta where the two great rivers come together and empty into the Persian Gulf. The mineral-rich silt runoff of the two rivers has left extremely rich and fertile land for growing crops though the region now receives very little annual rain. Because of the constant change of the runoff, it was necessary for the inhabitants to build dikes, canals and dams to keep the arable land free of floods. It is this area where mankind developed its first city states in what we now know as Ancient Sumer. And it is in this area that Abraham was born and lived in the city state of Ur in its Third Dynasty around the year 2000 BC. Many times we think of these ancient civilizations as very primitive and the inhabitants "just not quite as intelligent as we are today." After researching the ancient cultures of Sumer, Akkad and Assyria from as far back as 3500 BC to the time of Abraham fifteen hundred years later, it is clear that the technological advances these civilizations achieved during this time could not have occurred unless they had IQ's equal or close to ours today. We find evidence that indicate man made many tremendous discoveries in science and mathematics years before Abraham lived without the help of accumulated knowledge and computers.

The reason that this area of the world is so important to our study is that the societies developed a way of writing over five thousand years ago that

---

[47] Hindi and Buddhism total 20.9% of the World's religious population a/o 1970: "World Religion Database - International religious demographic statistics and sources": Todd M. Johnson, Ph.D., Brian J Grim, Ph.D., ed., Boston University

has come down to us today in a form we can easily decipher. This was a thousand years before hieroglyphics told the story of ancient Egypt, and we have yet to discover any Chinese or Indian ancient written history nearly this old. As we shall see, these discoveries have given Bible scholars an entirely new perspective on how Sacred Scripture has been handed down to us in the form we know today.

The Hebrew Nation

Even though Terah and Abraham were Semites, they were not yet a separate Hebrew nation. It seems to me that from what we find in Genesis, God's role for Abraham will be to establish the Hebrews into a separate religious and political entity within Mesopotamia. When we review the Abrahamic covenants, we will see that God's promise to Abraham is to make him *the father of a great nation,* while little is said of monotheism at this stage in God's Plan of Salvation.

Genesis makes it clear that Abraham and his descendants were well aware of the need to keep their clan free of other Semitic tribes. For this reason we see that both Abraham and Isaac send their servants from Canaan back to the town of Nahor in Aram Naharaim, near Haran in northern Mesopotamia, to find a wife for their sons as they did not want their family to marry into the Canaanites. Abraham's servant found Rebekah and brought her to Isaac. The town of Nahor could have been named after either Terah's father Nahor or Abraham's brother Nahor, who remained in Haran when Terah left the city state of Ur.[48] By keeping the progeny within the family of Terah, Abraham and Isaac maintained the pure line of Hebrew blood for their descendants, which was the first step in making the Hebrews a distinct Semitic people in Canaan. They will later be sealed with God by the covenant of circumcision, which will further distinguish them from their neighbors. Over many years, Abraham's people will suffer exile both in their slavery in Egypt and the Babylon captivity. These two events will force the Hebrew's to clan as one nation, as most immigrants in a foreign nation do to protect themselves and their culture. From this time forward the Hebrews, who by this time were called Jews, have been considered a separate race of Semites.

---

[48] Gen 24:10-61

The Beginning of Monotheism

Have you ever wondered why the God depicted in the Hebrew Scriptures seems to be somehow different than God the Father in the Gospels? Does it not seem that the God of the Hebrews has all the bad traits that we humans have? He even takes out His anger on mankind by punishing whole groups of people for the sin of one person. How is it that God's chosen people have a concept of God that is foreign to us today if Christianity is the fulfillment of the Law of Moses?[49] As God cannot change, there must be a human explanation. There is. **Anthropomorphism** refers to the perception of divine beings in human form, giving human qualities to these deities. As we will see in Chapter five, there are many Genesis-like stories found in the epic tales of ancient Mesopotamia. These ancient mythologies tell of gods, that like man, had vices and virtues such as jealousy, anger, rage, hatred, affection, lust and love. Anthropomorphism in this case is referred to as **Anthropotheism**. This understanding of deity was the norm in the early stages of Hebrew theology. Many of the gods *spread their seed* to both goddess and humans—many times forcefully. We find more than one god suffering from drunkenness, which was evidently a problem then as now. One is reminded of Noah getting drunk on wine after his covenant with God and passing out naked.[50] We see Yahweh with many of these same characteristics in early Judaism.

Ancient Mesopotamian religions were **Henotheistic** meaning that each city state or empire had one **primary** god of more importance than other deities as we find with the moon god *Sin* in Ur (the earlier home of Abraham). This was the norm in ancient Sumer and Akkad (3500-2500BC). This primary god was not necessarily superior in the pantheon, and the faithful could and did worship the other gods if they so choose. The other gods still had their duties to fulfill in the pantheon.

---

[49] Mt 5:17
[50] Gen 9:21

Monolatry, on the other hand, is the worship of one **superior** god while accepting the existence of the other gods in the pantheon.[51] In Mesopotamia as well as Canaan polytheism combined the responsibilities of the various gods by placing them under the direction of only one God. While this was a step away from the pure polytheism of ancient Sumer towards monotheism, it still was not the monotheism we know today. This **superior** god was still anthropomorphic and not a transcendent omnipotent God that the Jews will finally come to know fifteen hundred years later. Abraham will find the practice of monolatry when he arrives in Canaan at the beginning of the second millennium as we will see in Chapter 9 *The Gods of Canaan*. There he will find the god El is *the god most-high* of the Canaanites, but certainly not alone in the pantheon.

The understanding of monolatry is extremely important to the thesis of this work as there is considerable evidence and scholarly opinion that this was the form of theology practiced by Abraham and his progeny up until God's revelation to Moses on Mount Sinai that He was the only God to be worshiped. This monolatry will remain for some time in the Hebrew Scriptures as we see a thousand years after Abraham left Ur for Canaan when his descendant King David of Judah would write in two separate Psalms:

> **For the Lord is a great God, the great king over all the gods.**[52]

> **God rises in the divine council, gives judgment in the midst of the gods**[53]

When David says that *the Lord (Yahweh) is the king over all the gods*, he is implying an equality of substance of the other gods with Yahweh, even if they are the gods of other peoples. It is clear that David's people had not

---

[51] The concept of *Monolatry* is first seen in the works of Julius Wellhausen (May 17, 1844 – January 7, 1918) who was a German biblical scholar and orientalist, noted particularly for his contribution to scholarly understanding of the origin of the Pentateuch/Torah. He is credited with being one of the originators of the documentary hypothesis. (Wikipedia)

[52] Psalm 95: 3-4

[53] Psalm 82

yet recognized Yahweh as a transcendent, omnipotent God completely different from gods created in man's image.

Mark S. Smith, in Chapter Six of his book *The Early History of God*, describes the *Origins and Development of Israelite Monotheism* in four phases: *The period of the Judges, The First Half of the Monarchy, The Second half of the Monarchy,* and *The Exile.*[54] He shows clearly that monolatry was the norm in Israel up until the time of the *Exile*. He opines that at the height of the Jewish nation under Kings David and Solomon, Yahweh grew in stature due to the consistency of the Yahwistic practices in the whole extended kingdom. He states that like Marduk in Babylon, Yahweh became a nationalistic God which had the effect of marginalizing the local deities even if they were still sometimes incorporated into Yahwistic cult.

Eventually the northern kingdom of Israel broke away from Judah, was defeated by the Assyrians and taken into captivity becoming the ten lost tribes of Israel. The remaining two tribes of Judah and Benjamin became a small enclave of believers known as the Jews. Finally, even the Jews were taken into captivity in Babylon for seventy years. While in captivity they had no other way to retain the Hebrew culture that Abraham and Moses gave them than to clan together. This small group of faithful Jews was able to reject the gods of Mesopotamia for the one God, Yahweh. They became cohesive during this captivity to the point where they began to establish a true monotheism and a separate religion with just the one God, Yahweh. It seemed that as the Jews became smaller in number, they practiced a more pure and rigid monotheism. It was at this time that the *Babylonian Talmud* was written to establish the tradition of the Jewish religion and cement in their minds that their God was the only true God and that only He could save them. Most Biblical scholars will point to this time in history as when the Jews first embraced the monotheism that we practice today. A few hundred years after their return from captivity, the Jews came to recognize Yahweh as a transcendent, omnipotent being which separated them from polytheism forever. This transition was assisted by something new to the Near East, the discipline of philosophy. After Alexander the Great conquered Palestine, the Jews were influenced by Hellenistic philosophers who denied human traits to their gods. The Greek philosopher Xenophanes said:

---

[54] Smith/History, Pgs. 182-199

"The greatest god resembles man neither in form nor in mind".[55]

As Hellenism was incorporated into Hebrew theology, anthropotheism gave way to a transcendent God who was above the contrivance and stratagem of men. The philosopher Karl Jaspers describes this time as the *Axial Age* in world history (800-200 BC) when there was an emergence of a revolutionary new human awareness of the separation between transcendent and mundane spheres of reality. This development was of paramount importance to the evolution of monotheism into what we see today. It seems that God in His wisdom knew that only a small but cohesive race of people could overcome the forces of secularism around them to develop the monotheism necessary for His Plan of Salvation to be fulfilled. Then, and only then, could that same nation's *anointed one of God*, whom the Greeks would call the *Christ*, come to mankind in the form of man in the Incarnation which was to be and still is the greatest event in the history of mankind.

---

[55] Xenophanes of Colophon in ancient Greece (570-475 BC) was a Greek philosopher, theologian, poet, and social and religious critic. Wikipedia

CHAPTER TWO

ANCIENT SUMER

Cush became the father of Nimrod, who was the first to become a mighty warrior on earth. He was a mighty hunter in the eyes of the Lord; hence the saying, "Like Nimrod, a mighty hunter in the eyes of the Lord." His kingdom originated in Babylon, Erech and Accad, all of them, in the land of Shinar.[56]

The Shinar of the Hebrew Scriptures is the ancient civilization known today as Sumer. It flourished during the *Bronze Age* of human history. The period of history called the Bronze Age is separated into three parts. The Early Bronze Age from 3300-2100 BC covered the time of Ancient Ur in Sumer, the Middle Bronze age from 2100-1550 is when Terah and Abraham lived in the Third Dynasty of Ur; and the late Bronze Age from 1550-1200 which ushered in the early Iron Age at the time of David. Before we follow Terah and his clan north from the city-state of Ur to the town of Haran to the north, it is extremely important to have a clear understanding of the culture, milieu and society of the Middle Bronze Age if we are to realize just how momentous God's call to Abraham was in this time of history. For this reason we will spend considerable time and effort to learn about the ancient civilizations of Sumer and Akkad and

---

[56] Gen 10:8-10 (Nimrod was possibly Tukulti-Ninurta I 13th Century BC) First Assyrian conqueror of Babylon and a famous city-builder. (NAB Footnotes)

particularly the Third Dynasty of Ur. This will help us understand the highly advanced society that Abraham lived when he was called by God.

The first great society of southern Mesopotamia was Sumer, which was known to historians to have flourished from approximately 3,800 to 1,750 BC although it could be older as the ageing techniques were not precise at the time this civilization was discovered. Archeologists have found evidence that a people called the *Ubaidians*, a non-Semitic people, established Sumer as far back as 6500 BC. This culture is named after the locale where the archeological dig was found.[57] The Sumerians are distinct by their writings and dialects. Some linguists claim that the name of the Tigris and Euphrates rivers and some Sumerian cities suggests a relationship of the Sumerians with an earlier civilization near Armenia on the Caspian Sea. As we shall see when we discover the history of the *deluge* in Genesis, other authors opine the Ubaidians came from the Black Sea area in what is now southern Turkey.[58] For over a thousand years before Terah left *Ur of the Chaldeans*, also known as *Ur Kasdim* by the Hebrews, the Sumerians were a distinct race of people, possessing their own unique language and culture, building and expanding history's first recorded city-states in the southern part of Mesopotamia. The *Chaldeans* themselves were not known to history until a thousand years later; however, this was the descriptive name of the city of Ur at the time the Hebrew Scriptures were reduced to writing in the form we know today. The main city-states of Ancient Sumer besides Ur were Eridu, Uruk (in Genesis Erech), Larsa, Adab, Umma, Lagash, Kish and the holy city of Nippur.

---

[57] The Ubaid civilization (ca. 6500-3800 BC) derives its name from the *tell* (mound) found near the town of *al-Ubaid,* which is just west of ancient Ur in southern Iraq's Dhi Qar province where Henry Hall and Leonard Woolley made the first discovery of this culture in 1927. *Hall, Henry R. and Woolley, C. Leonard.* 1927. Al-'Ubaid. Ur Excavations. Oxford: Oxford University Press

[58] Ian Wilson, *Before the Flood, The Biblical Flood as a real event and how it changed the course of civilization.* (New York: St. Martin's Press, 2001) (hereafter Wilson)

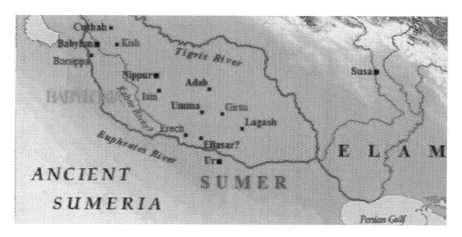

Archeologists have found thousands of artifacts of Sumerian civilization carved on temple walls, outside of and within the great Ziggurat temples (which means Holy Mountain), on stone steles which were used to tell tales of victory and valor of the kings, and on *circular seals* artistically carved to tell ancient epic stories. The most informative documents for historians has been found on over 250,000 clay tablets in the cuneiform language left thousands of years ago in their libraries, palaces and temples. Every year there are thousands of additional tablets discovered that enhance our understanding of this incredible ancient culture.

Cuneiform writing

The Sumerians, like the Romans two thousand years later, were great keepers of administrative and commercial records. Ancient Sumer kept theirs on tablets written with a triangle tipped stylus, in a unique language called *cuneiform*, which they put on soft clay tablets hardened by fire to be made permanent. Cuneiform is from the Latin meaning wedge-shaped and is history's first written language, although not yet an alphabet. The main reason it was so successful was that for the first time in recorded history, its symbols represented *sounds* that could be combined into words rather than a pictograph or idea common to Egyptian hieroglyphics – which is similar to our own highway signs today.

As we can see from the chart here, early Sumerian writings were also pictograph but over time evolved into a form that was easily written with a standard stylus.[59] Egyptian hieroglyphics were developed at about the same time but did not evolve into this easily written form. Cuneiform was used throughout the ancient Middle East for thousands of years as can be seen by the Tell el-Amarna tablets written in cuneiform by the Egyptians to communicate with their provinces in Canaan and Syria in 1460 BC. This language was originally discovered in the late eighteenth century in the ancient Persian tablet known as the *Persepolis* – a trilingual inscription similar to the Rosetta stone in Egypt – but written in cuneiform. One of the unknown languages on the stone was Sumerian. Deciphering this piece eventually led historians to discover Sumer as a separate and ancient civilization in Mesopotamia.[60] Certainly the ancient Egyptians, Chinese and Indian civilizations made records of their history. Unfortunately, their documents were most likely placed on dissolvable materials such as parchments or papyri; therefore, we find few extant records from these cultures. For this reason, these cuneiform clay tablets are the most ancient extant archives of historical events. As we shall see later, cuneiform will be enhanced into an alphabet by the people in Ugarit in northern Canaan about the time that Abraham enters that country. Ugaritic cuneiform will lead to an alphabetic

3000 BC	2800 BC	2500 BC	1800 BC	600 BC	
					an (god, heaven)
					ki (earth)
					lu (man)
					sal (woman/female)
					kur (mountain, land)
					geme (female slave)
					sag (head)
					ka (mouth)
					ninda (bread)

---

[59] Source: http://pandora.cii.wwu.edu/vajda/ling201/writingsystems/sumeriancuneiform.htm

[60] Samuel Noah Kramer, *The Sumerians: Their History, Culture, and Character* (Chicago, University of Chicago Press, 1971) pg. 6 (Hereafter Kramer/Sumerians)

based Hebrew language, which will further distinguish the Hebrew people from other Semites. It is also the reason that the Hebrews have such a long historical record. Without the alphabet from the Sumerians through Ugarit, there may not have been a Hebrew written language until much later in their history.

Geopolitical Sumer

Geography plays an important part in the success and longevity of a civilization. The fact that Sumer was located along two major rivers and the Persian Gulf gave them an ample amount of fresh water, easy transportation and extremely fertile land to grow crops. This allowed them to meld their people into the world's first city-states. These early city-states evolved a very effective political system with extensive infrastructure, administration and defenses. In the early days of Sumer the political authority was held by the citizens. Each city-state had an assembly consisting of *elders* in an upper house and a lower house of *men* who elected a city-governor known as an *ensi*.[61] As conflicts between city-states increased, military governors assumed more control, eventually leading to monarchs who passed on power to their family leading to dynasties. In the Hebrew Scriptures we see the same progression of political power where each tribe elected elders or *Judges* to rule (both male and female). As the tribes became less able to defend themselves from the Canaanites around them, they eventually chose to elect a king to rule them knowing full well that it would mean giving up individual liberties that they then held.[62] As we have learned from these narratives, they had the prophet Samuel anoint Saul as their first king. This political reality is repeated in the Greek and Roman republics as well and seems to be the life cycle of all democratic forms of government throughout history.

The ancient cities of Sumer were built on raised ground to avoid floods. In the last stages of Sumer, they built huge Ziggurat temples dedicated to the local god. These temples became extremely important within the society. The priests and caretakers of the temple held high social status and lived on the temple grounds. The temple itself was like a corporation and owned a

---

[61] Ibid, pg. 74

[62] I Sm 8: 1-22

large portion of the land surrounding it, including some agricultural lands that the priests rented to share cropper type of commoners. Most scholars of ancient Sumer assumed that the temple leaders and the monarchy owned and controlled most of the land. The Russian Sumerian scholar I.M. Diakanoff posits that there were four classes of landed people in Sumerian society: nobles, commoners, clients, and slaves. According to Diakanoff:

1) The *nobles* owned large private estates that they passed on to their heirs and made up most of the upper house of elders.
2) The *commoners* owned their own private plot of land in the name of the family which too could be inherited. It was the commoners who probably made up the lower house of the bicameral assembly.
3) The *clients* were the merchants, smiths, artisans, scribes and those that worked for the temple, the nobility and the government. They were the middle class without landed estates.
4) The *slaves* were a legally recognized class who were owned by the temple, palace and nobility and considered chattel which could be bought and sold. A commoner in debt could sell himself or members of his family into three-year slavery to pay off his debt and then work separately to purchase their freedom. [63]

Genesis says that Terah was an owner of slaves in Ur and Haran. Therefore, we can assume from Diakanoff's theory that Terah and Abraham were either nobility or landed commoners in Ur. We know from extant documents from Sumer that the nobility and commoner classes were highly educated and literate; however, a formal education was only available for those that could afford to pay the tuition at the schools for scribes where they learned to read and write the cuneiform system. This was proven by a German cuneiformist, Nickolaus Schneider, who discovered and listed the occupations of the fathers of the scribe students in the schools in Ur in 2000 BC, which is just about the time that Abraham was growing up there. This list included many of what we would consider upper middle income or professional occupations such as:

Governors, ambassadors, temple administrators, military and
naval officers, tax officials, priests, managers, supervisor's

---

[63] Diakanoff, *Sumer: Society and State in Ancient Mesopotamia* (Moscow, 1959) from Kramer/Sumer, pg. 75

foremen, scribes, archivists and accountants. In short, their fathers were the wealthiest citizens of urban communities.[64]

Notwithstanding Diakanoff's limited theory, the city-states also had farmers who grew and stored grain and raised domesticated cattle and oxen. We have found pictures of farmers milking cows, making butter to store and using ox driven plows with seed dispensers attached. There is extant a *farmer's almanac* that gives detailed instructions for the proper methods and time to plant. Being located on two major rivers and a series of canals, boatmen and fishermen were plentiful, and the Sumerians were the first to invent the fish farm for commercial use. There were merchants, scribes, lawyers and doctors, architects, stone masons and carpenters, smiths, jewelers and potters. The workers were paid with money in the form of a disk of silver of standard weight. Later in its history they used silver rods of exact weight where a merchant could clip off an exact measured amount for a purchase.[65] Each city had a defensive wall with the peasant population living outside the walls in reed huts in small cities and villages. Most of the houses within the city were two and three stories built with fire hardened brick and mortar (usually bitumen). Not all cities were rich enough to have a Ziggurat.

Sumerian Culture

Sumer's city-states had long and storied literary achievements including the legendary *Epic of Gilgamesh,* which was written fifteen centuries before Homer's epics – although not to be compared. This was an advanced and thriving civilization; and because they have left us a written record, we know that they were one of the first to cultivate land with intricate irrigation systems. They also developed a system of extensive canals which had adjacent roads where oxen teams pulled commercial laden boats up and down the canals and rivers. Some of these canals are still being used today in Iraq. The Sumerians were the first to record the use of wheeled vehicles in about 2500 BC, which were at first two axle vehicles pulled by

---

[64] Samuel Noah Kramer, *History begins at Sumer: Thirty-Nine Firsts in recorded history* (Penn, University of Penn Press, 1956) pg. 5 (Hereafter, Kramer/History)

[65] Gwendolyn Leick, *Mesopotamia, The Invention of the City* (England, Penguin Books, 2001), pg. 125 (Hereafter Leick)

donkeys or oxen. By 1800 BC, the war wagon had evolved into a single axle *spoke whee*l vehicle drawn by horses called the chariot.[66] The chariot was first used in northern Mesopotamia by the Hittites and was the first use of the horse in war. Single horse mounted soldiers were hundreds of years later. As we shall see later, Western Semites, called Hyksos, will introduce this same single axle chariot to Egypt in the about 1750 BC.

The Sumerians left us written instructions on how to cultivate several wild grains into agricultural cereals. Recently archeologists discovered that as early as the seventh millennium BC, inhabitants of northern Mesopotamia were able to domesticate strains of wild wheat into a variety that was more conducive to produce seeds that could better be thrashed into grain.[67] This knowledge may have come with the Ubaidians when they entered the river delta of southern Mesopotamia. Ur itself was a center of commerce and was known in particular for its fine woven textiles of linen and wool, some of which may have come from some of Terah's sheep if indeed that was part of his livelihood. During Ur III the textile industry of wool and linen clothing was administered by the state, which kept detailed administrative documents showing a very centralized government that controlled the work force. Because Sumer had no natural forests or mineral deposits, it was forced to trade its cereals, bronze goods, leather and fine woven textiles with most of the known world. They would trade them for the ores that made their metals and wood from the forests of the mountains of Elam (Persia). We still have records of these transactions using the merchant's circular seals, which identified the products and their destinations which were mostly along the Tigris and Euphrates but also as far as Egypt and the Indian sub-continent.

The Sumerians were advanced in mathematics using a 60 base place–value number system, which allowed them to record very small and large numbers and which gave us the 360 degree circle and the 60 minute hour. They had

---

[66] The invention of the chariot in the steppe (southern Russian plains) - perhaps originally meant as an improved tool for hunting - occurred roughly by 2000 BC, probably in the area just east of the southern Ural mountains, where the oldest chariots have been unearthed. The word for horse appears just around this date for the first time in Mesopotamia, when an increase in north-south trade through Iran is attested. (Ancient History Encyclopedia)

[67] Wilson, Before the Flood, Chapter 7, *the First Geneticists*.

the ability to determine square roots and cubes of numbers up to 32 and it appears that they had determined the equivalent of pi. There is the famous *Plimpton 322 clay tablet* from 1800 BC in Ur III that some mathematicians opine was equal to the Pythagorean Theorem of right angled triangles. Some Greek mathematicians are not so sure. They had determined the areas of rectangles, triangles and trapezoids, and the volumes of bricks and cylinders.[68] They used their advanced mathematics to predict astronomical occurrences such as solar and lunar eclipses. More important to historians and astronomers, they recorded these eclipses for centuries leading to the *Enuma Anu Enlil,*[69] which is the oldest extant astronomical text. The Sumerians wrote the first calendars, established standard weights and measures, and archeologists found an abacus in their ruins.

Politically the city-states holdings were separated into provinces ruled by an *ensi* who was responsible for keeping the peace and collecting taxes. There are several extant documents showing very detailed property lines between cities and states, some of which were the formal peace treaties of armed conflicts over borders. They had a well-developed legal system with precedent setting court cases, documented marriage and adoption contracts, divorce settlements and the purchase, lease and sale of property. The Sumerians had a very strong concept of private property, the sale of which they documented on clay tablets signed by the parties with personal *circular seals* that they would roll onto the soft clay. Archeologists have found a tablet that recorded the sale of just one sheep. There is a very interesting little story translated from a document found near the town of Dilbad just south of what is Bagdad of today that documents not only a lease of land but one to a man named *Abrahama*:

> "Concerning the 400 shars of land, the field of Sin-idinam which to Abrahama to lease ... ..."[70]

---

[68] From: http://www.storyofmathematics.com/sumerian.html

[69] Enuma Anu Enlil (literal translation: *When the gods Anu and Enlil*) is a major series of 68 or 70 tablets dealing with Babylonian astrology. The bulk of the work is a substantial collection of omens, estimated to number between 6500 and 7000, which interpret a wide variety of celestial and atmospheric phenomena in terms relevant to the king and state. Wikipedia

[70] George A. Barton, *Historical Value of the Patriarchal Narratives, Proceedings of the American Philosophical Society, 52, April 1,* 1913,) pg. 196, (Hereafter Barton)

This would be a great find for Bible scholars if this was Abraham the patriarch. But it was not, as this Abrahama is identified as the son of another man. However, this lease was written about the time that Abraham lived in Ur, and it shows that Abraham was a common name in that time and place. This concept of purchasing private property would be important to Abraham when he attempted to pay for a parcel of land to bury his wife Sarah in Canaan. The Canaanite owner (identified as a Hittite) offers several times to give the property to him but Abraham insists on paying a set amount of silver for the field in *Machpelah facing Mamre*, which is near Hebron. We see that he documents the sale. If Abraham was of nobility status in Ur and therefore literate, he certainly would continue the practice of documenting land transactions as was practiced in the Sumerian and Akkadian culture, even though it seemed unnecessary to the people of Canaan. Genesis documents the transaction:

> ***Abraham accepted Ephron's terms; he weighed out to him the silver that Ephron had stipulated in the hearing of the Hittites, four hundred shekels of silver at the current market value. Thus Ephron's field in Machpelah, facing Mamre, together with its cave and all the trees anywhere within its limits, was conveyed to Abraham by purchase in the presence of the Hittites, all who entered the gate of Ephron's city.***[71]

Abraham passed this concept on to his heirs. Hundreds of years later, during the time of the Kings in Israel, Ahab the King of Samaria wanted a neighboring vineyard owned by Naboth. Because Naboth refused to sell it to him, the king was forced to have Naboth wrongly accused and stoned to death before he could take the property. Most monarchs, outside of Mesopotamia, had complete control of all property and would not have had to resort to perjury as we observed King Ahab do to obtain Naboth's vineyard in I Kings.[72]

---

[71] Gen 23:16-18

[72] I Kings 21:1-16

CHAPTER THREE

EMPIRE -- AKKAD AND UR III

"I am Naram-Sin, King of the four corners of the world"

The Semitic peoples who lived in the central and northern parts of Mesopotamia along the Tigris and Euphrates rivers were known as the Akkadians and would later become the Babylonians and Assyrians. The people of the city of Agade, the principal city of the Semites in Mesopotamia, were known as the *Agadians* on the extant documents that archaeologists have discovered. However, Genesis refers to them as Accad, while historians now use Akkad for this civilization.[73] The Akkadian language, which was clearly of a Semitic derivative and different from that of Sumer, was the universal language of commerce throughout the Near East all the way into Egypt and India for over a thousand years. The Akkadians eventually conquered the city-states of Sumer and assimilated them into the Akkadian society. This caused the Sumerians, as a separate people, to disappear from history.

In the third millennium BC, an Akkadian King, *Sargon the Great*[74] united most of the Near East into what some historians have called the world's first great empire. Most records say he reined from 2270 to 2215 BC, but the early king lists are suspect. Sargon gave us detailed descriptions

---

[73] Gen 10:10

of himself and his military conquests; therefore, we have considerable information about his reign. According to the *Legend of Sargon*:

> "Sargon, the mighty king, king of Agad am I. My mother was a high priestess, my father I knew not. ... ... My mother, the high priestess, conceived me, in secret she bore me. She set me in a basket of rushes; with bitumen she sealed my lid. She cast me into the river which rose not over me. The river bore me up and carried me to Akki, the drawer of water. ... ... Akki, the drawer of water took me as his son and reared me."[75]

Where have we heard this story before? This is one more example of an ancient narrative that may have found its way into the Hebrew Scriptures, as Sargon I was well documented in Akkadian literature and would have been well known to Abraham. Interestingly enough, Sargon's namesake Sargon II, will capture the Samaritans of the northern kingdom of Israel in 721 BC, and deport them back to his country where they will become *the ten lost tribes of Israel*. [76] On one of Sargon II's victory steles he states:

> "At the beginning of my rule ... the city of the Samarians (Samaritans) I besieged and conquered ... Carried off as prisoner 27,290 of the people who dwelled in it." [77]

The fact that the Hebrews of Samaria were taken back to a land from which they originally came could well account for the reason that so few returned to Israel. The same can be said of the Judeans taken to Babylon a hundred years later as the Book of Ezra tells us, only 42,360 Judeans returned to Israel when they had the chance.[78]

Sargon's grandson, Naram-Sin (2254-2218 BC), claimed to have extended Sargon's empire all the way from the Upper Sea (the Mediterranean) into

---

[75] Pritchard, pg. 119, The Legend of Sargon
[76] II Kings 17:5-6
[77] Documents from Old Testament Times, Thomas, D.W. ed. (New York: Harper & Row, 1958)
[78] Ezra 2:64)

the Taurus and Amanus mountains of southern Turkey as far as Armenia to below the Lower Sea to what was called the land of Silver in the Arabian Peninsula. He even turned the city of Susa in Elam into a vassal-state. In an expansive mood, Naram-Sin claimed on the stele that he was king of the four corners of the world – a claim made by more than one empire builder in Mesopotamia. Records show that Naram-Sin traded with the people of *Meluhha*, which some scholars believe is located in the Indus Valley in what is now Pakistan.[79] Naram-Sin eventually captured the fortified city of Ur by force after a long siege causing great bloodshed and terror within the city.

A team of archeologists and soil scientists led by Dr. Harvey Weiss of Yale University has recently discovered that there was a drastic climate change in central and northern Mesopotamia beginning in 2200 BC that lasted for 300 years. There is archeological evidence of abandonment of major cities in the north and migration of Semites to the south. According to Dr. Weiss, these migrations doubled the population of the southern cities causing food and water shortages, which may have led to the collapse of the Sargon Dynasties.[80] This drought would have ended just about the time that Terah chose to leave Ur for Haran.

At the last stages of the Naram-Sin's dynasty, from 2190 to 2115 BC, there was an invasion of all Mesopotamia by the *Gutian* "barbarians from the north" who came out of the Zagros Mountains northeast of Akkad from near where the Kurds are today in southern Turkey and Iraq, probably caused by the same drought. They captured and plundered the city of Agade and ravaged most of Sumer with hit and run raids, making most of the cities of Sumer and Akkad vassal-states. This destruction was well documented in a historiographical poem entitled *The Curse of Agade, The*

---

[79] The civilization was called the Harappa: "The site of the ancient city contains the ruins of a Bronze Age fortified city, which was part of the Cemetery H culture and the Indus Valley Civilization, centered in Sindh and the Punjab. The city is believed to have had as many as 23,500 residents and occupied over 100 hectares (250 acres) at its greatest extent during the Mature Harappan phase (2600–1900 BC), which is considered large for its time." Brian Fagan, Nadia Durrani, *People of the earth: an introduction to world prehistory.* (2003) pg. 414.

[80] "Collapse Linked to Drought", By John Noble Wilford, NY Times, 24 August 1993

Ekur Avenged Saga, parts of which we see below. It claims that Naram-Sin was being punished by the god Enlil for desecrating the temple to Enlil in the holy city of Nippur some time earlier. This tale gives us one of the few insights into the culture and civilized nature of the Sumerians when it describes the horror the barbarous Gutians brought to a highly civilized society:

> "--- and brought down the Gutians, a people which brooks no controls; it covered the earth like the locust, so that none could escape its power. Communications, whether by land or by sea, became impossible throughout Sumer; the herald could not proceed on his journey; the sea-rider could not sail his boat ------; brigands dwelt on the roads; the doors of the gates of the land turned to clay; all the surrounding lands were planning evil on the city walls"[81]

The author of this poem gives us some idea of how a superior and well established culture abhorred the barbarity of the invading peoples. Certainly they were used to wars with each other but evidently these barbarians did not respect their cultured sensibilities. This same situation is repeated 2500 years later when the superior culture of Rome is shocked when Rome is sacked by the "barbarians from the north" in Europe. We bring this up to give an insight into how Terah and his family might have felt that their society was disintegrating and to emphasize that Abraham was brought up in a highly cultured society for this time in history. This, combined with the economic hardships of Ur III, gives clear reasons for a man of means to migrate away from hardship to better opportunities.

The Third Dynasty of Ur

As a result of the abandonment of the Akkadian cities in the north, the city-state of Ur had a renaissance about the time that Terah and his family lived there. During this dynasty, Ur-Nammu, an ensi working for King Utu-hegal, who was credited with driving out the Gutians, may have usurped the throne and established the so called Third Dynasty of Ur

---

[81] Kramer/Sumerians pg. 62-64

or Ur III, which controlled much of Mesopotamia between 2113 and 2004 BC. They ruled over most of Mesopotamian from the northern mountains of Anatolia (southern Turkey of today) to the Persian Gulf. The surrounding vassal states fluctuated frequently.

Like the Roman Empire two thousand years later, the cement that held the empire together was its highly developed bureaucracy run by a well-trained cadre of civil servants established by Ur Nammu's son, Shulgi. Shulgi established written administration procedure for the entire empire and left us documents showing a standard tax system and calandar throughout the empire.[82] This advanced civil service was as important to keeping the empire together as a large military presence. It was during this time that the dynasty developed the horse driven chariot and other weapons superior to their neighbors. Shulgi was one of the few kings in Mesopotamia that was deified during his lifetime. Ur-Nammu and his son Shulgi reigned for over sixty years. During that time they stabilized Ur III into a relatively long period of peace, and it was during this time that the great Ziggurats at Ur and Uruk were built.

During the reign of Shulgi's sons, Amar-Su'ema, Shu-Sin and Ibi-Sin, we find the first serious problems within the Third Dynasty. Ibi-Sin was a weak leader that one of his generals said was hated by the god Enlil due to bad omens proven from the examination of sacrificed animals. I guess this was the style of political hit for this time in history. During this time there was also a famine in Ur III, and the price of grain increased causing inflation and eventual financial ruin of the empire. This caused many cities-states to break away so that they could fend for themselves.[83] As they broke away, the empire lost tax revenue, which means they could not afford to pay for an army to protect their holdings.

It was at this time that we find the first incursions into Ur III by the Amorites, a Semitic people who came out of the desert of Syria and Canaan west of Ur III, probably during the drought of 2200 BC in northern Mesopotamia, gaining control of many Sumero-Akkadian cities such as Isin, Larsa and Kish. They established the city-state of Babylon, which came to be ruled by Hammurabi and eventually will be known as the Assyrians. We see a lot of

---

[82] Leick, pg. 123

[83] Kramer/Sumerians, pg. 68-70

the Amorites mentioned in the Hebrew Scriptures. Sihon and Og, whom Moses will defeat on his way to Canaan,[84] were Kings of the Amorites from the Dead Sea Area. The Amorite invasions were followed by attacks from the Elamite Awan kings to the east, causing considerable disintegration of the Ur III dynasty. We shall visit the Awan kings again when we find Abraham involved in the *four kings against five* incidents in Genesis.

The Jewish *Seder Olam Rabbah* states that Abram, the son of Terah, was born in 1976 BC. This record assumes the extremely long lifetimes of the ancient patriarchs and is therefore suspect; however, by back dating from the relatively certain dates of the patriarchs in Canaan and Egypt, most Bible scholars today agree that Abraham was born about 2000 BC. This would have Terah and his clan leaving Ur III at about the time that the dynasty was declining. It therefore seems quite possible that Terah took advantage of the time of peace during the reign of Shulgi or his sons to move from Ur to Haran.

The Code of Ur-Nammu

The existence of a strong bureaucracy in the Third Dynasty led to the set of written laws that were formalized into the Code of Ur-Nammu, which is considered the earliest written law codes in history. This set of laws predated the infamous Hammurabi code of 1772 BC by over three hundred years. The Ur-Nammu codes dealt mostly with contract law regarding marriage, slavery, adoption, business regulations and personal injury, but also specified fines for criminal acts such as theft and burglary. As women were not considered equal to men, the laws included capital punishments for her infidelities, while at worst the men suffered monetary fines for the same offense. Most compensation was in the form of specified amounts of shekels of silver and differed according to the class of the subjects. A few examples of the Ur-Nammu code that follow give a sample of the morality and culture of the time.

> "If the wife of a man, by employing her charms, followed after another man and he slept with her, they (the

---

[84] Dt 31:4

authorities) shall slay that woman, but that other man shall be set free."[85]

This chauvinism is quite similar to current Sharia Law. And then we find:

> "If a man had accused another man of … and he (the accuser) had him brought to the river-ordeal, and the river ordeal proved him innocent, then the man who had brought the accuser must pay him three shekels of silver."[86]

We can only speculate what the *river-ordeal* entailed. Also extant are the Laws of Lipit-Istar (1934-1924 BC), the Laws of Dadusha (1800 BC) and the famous Hammurabi Code. The Hammurabi Code (aka Hammurapi Code) consisted of 282 laws including criminal matters such as murder, robbery assault and bodily injuries. The laws were enforced by an ensi or magistrates, but only the king could rule on crimes or actions punishable by death.[87]

According to Maimonides, the great Jewish intellectual rabbi of the 12th century, the Torah lists 613 separate laws with punishments given by Moses for the Hebrews. There are many parallels in the Hammurabi Code with laws and punishments outlined in Chapters 21-23 of Exodus, Chapters 17-12 of Leviticus and Chapters 12-26 in Deuteronomy. For instance the first law listed in the Code of Hammurabi concerns the punishment for wrongly accusing another:

> "If a seignior (man/citizen) accused another seignior and brought a charge of murder against him, but was not proved, his accuser shall be put to death." [88]

In the story of Susanna in the book of Daniel, we see a similar result once Daniel exposed the two men who wrongly accused Susanna …

---

[85] Pritchard, The Laws of Ur-Nammu, pg. 524

[86] Ibid.

[87] *Readings from the Ancient near East – Primary Sources of Old Testament Study*, ed. Bill T. Arnold, Bryan E. Beyer (Michigan, Baker Academic, 2002) Chapter Six, *Law Codes* (Hereafter Arnold/Beyer)

[88] Pritchard, The Code of Hammurabi, pg. 166

They rose up against the two old men, for by their own words Daniel had convicted them of bearing false witness. They condemned them to the fate they had planned for their neighbor. [89]

In the ancient Near Eastern codes, there is a clear distinction of the class of person involved. If a person of higher class damages a person of a lower class, there can be a monetary fine; but if the opposite is true, the punishment for the lower class person could be dismemberment or death. The Hammurabi Code is where we first see the idea of *eye for an eye and a tooth for a tooth* being codified as we see below:

> "If a seignior has destroyed the eye of a member of the aristocracy, they shall destroy his eye. If he has broken another seignior's bone, they shall break his bone. If he has destroyed the eye of a commoner or broken the bone of a commoner, he shall pay one mina of silver." [90]

It would appear that justice was not the prime motivation of the ancient laws as much as equitable reparations and reprisals. That is because these laws were written by men for man to better control his environment. On the other hand, the Hebrew Scriptures, because they are inspired by the Holy Spirit, also consider the victim – adding morality to the mandates as well as an obligation to worship God as seen below in Leviticus:

You shall not exploit your neighbor. You shall not commit robbery. You shall not withhold overnight the wages of your laborer. You shall not insult the deaf, or put a stumbling block in front of the blind, but you shall fear your God. I am the Lord. ----- Take no revenge and cherish no grudge against your own people. You shall love your neighbor as yourself. I am the Lord. [91]

---

[89] Dan 13: 61
[90] Pritchard, The Code of Hammurabi, pg. 175
[91] Lev 19:13-14, 18

While the Mesopotamian law codes are interesting to us, God's call to mankind in the Torah and the Gospels *to treat your neighbor as yourself* is what separates Jews and Christians from secular laws and practices. And, as we shall see in the next chapter, Terah was not alone in his *worship of other gods.* In fact, the entire known world at this time worshiped a pantheon of pagan gods. That is why it is important for us to grasp just how momentous God's call to Abraham was at this time in history. We shall see when Abraham moves into Canaan, monotheism will not come easy to this pagan world.

Chapter Four

THE GODS OF MESOPOTAMIA

"The Sumerians, according to their own records, cherished goodness and truth, law and order, justice and freedom, righteousness and straightforwardness, mercy and compassion. And they abhorred evil and falsehood, lawlessness and disorder, injustice and oppression, sinfulness and perversity, cruelty and pitilessness."[92]

As we recall from Chapter 1, Joshua tells us that ***Terah served other gods***. What Joshua did not tell us is what kind of other gods Terah served and how he served them. What kind of religion did his family practice? At the head of this chapter I have quoted Samuel Noel Kramer because as one of the world's foremost authorities on ancient Sumer[93], he knew the people as well as anyone could from four thousand years away. It is easy for us to think that a polytheist must somehow be evil with no moral code. If Kramer's analysis of the people of Abraham's time is correct, then we can see that Terah and Abraham could be righteous in the eyes of God even if they had not yet come to understand His omnipotence.

In ancient Sumer we find the world's first written record of a formalized religion. Religion is defined as *a set of beliefs concerning the cause, nature*

---

[92] Kramer/History pg. 102

[93] Kramer's translations of many of the Sumerian myths and epics are included in the Pritchard book of *Ancient Near Eastern Texts*

and purpose of the universe – containing a moral code governing the conduct of human affairs.[94] Ancient Mesopotamian polytheists did worship a pantheon of gods, who they believed were the cause, nature, and purpose of the universe.[95] Their gods had a set of beliefs about creation and a moral code recorded in the mythology and epic stories we will review in Chapter 5. The ancient Sumero-Akkadian polytheism included over 2100 male and female gods in their mythology.[96] They believed that the gods were animate beings who affected every aspect of their lives which was reflected in their laws, customs and rituals. Their gods were not transcendent, supernatural ultimate beings as we understand God today. Their gods were created in man's imagination and therefore were in man's image with a time and place in history. The gods were a little above man and seemed to have the same traits and habits. There is a hierarchy of gods within the pantheon with minor gods serving the more important gods. The primary deity in the pantheon usually had a consort, who begat other gods who were given specific responsibilities such as bringing rain, preventing famines, giving a good harvest, helping in love and war, agriculture, medicine, and even for supervising morality.

Gods of Sumer & Akkad

In the earliest *god lists* of ancient Sumer, we find four main gods who dominated the pantheon. The heaven-god **Anu** (also called **An**), the air-god **Enlil**, the water-god **Enki**, and the great mother-goddess **Ninhursag**. These four gods are often seen together as an assembly directing the other gods. The ancient god *Anu* seemed to be the supreme god in the early years of Sumer because he was the god of the first known city-state of Uruk (Ereck in Genesis). The Sumerian word for the universe is *An-Ki*, which is derived from the god *Anu* (An) and the goddess **Ki,** who early in their history begot the pantheon of gods of Sumer. As time passed, Anu faded away; and his

---

[94] Dictionary.com

[95] *Ancient Mesopotamian polytheism* in this context is dated from the early Uruk age of 3500 BC up to the time of Ur III in 2000 BC.

[96] Jean Bottero (30 August 1914 – 15 December 2007) a French historian and Assyriologist estimates there were over 2100 separate deities in ancient Mesopotamian polytheism. He wrote several books on Ancient Near East Religions including *The Birth of God* and *Everyday life in ancient Mesopotamia*.

son, the air-god Enlil, became dominant in the pantheon of Sumer. Enlil is referred to as *the father of the gods* and *the King of heaven and earth.*

Enki, the Sumerian *water god* and the *god of wisdom*, was the father image deity of Sumer depicted as old, gray-haired and retired. Thanks to Michelangelo, we Christians picture God the Father in the same gray-haired strong-willed manner as the god Enki is depicted in ancient Sumer. Enki, while the head of the pantheon in many cases, was not a creating deity because Nammu is mentioned as the mother of Enki in some stories. As we shall see in the *Chaos of Creation* myth of Akkad, the god **Apsu** is called the *begetter*. Enki's equivalent, as the superior god of the pantheon, will be known as Ea in Akkadian lore; and as we will see later; will be known as **El** in Canaanite Ugaritic theology. Enki was not only the water god but the god of *fresh water*, the water of life – which is shown flowing up from the earth in the reliefs found on ancient temple walls. The goddess of salt water is not held in the same esteem and is frequently at odds with Enki. This is quite understandable for a society living in the marshlands where the Tigris and Euphrates rivers enter into the Persian Gulf as brine water, which frequently damaged the crops of Sumer.

The mother-goddess Ninhursag was called the *Exalted Lady* and the *Lady of the Mountain.*[97] One temple hymn identifies *her as the true and great lady of heaven.* She was the goddess of fertility for the ancient Sumerian cities of Adab and Kish. In early god-lists she ranked above Enki and in one story created mankind from clay. Early in Sumer she was called the goddess of mother-earth and was shown as an early consort of Anu, the god of heaven where her job was to usher in the spring. It is probable that the Ubaidians came from the Caspian or Black Sea area, both of which had a dominant mother goddess as their primary deity as far back as 7,000 BC, which could be the reason that the Sumerians gave goddesses greater standing than gods early in their history.[98] As the Akkadian Semites assimilated into Sumerian society, gods became primary, and goddesses become consorts or goddesses of fertility. The Akkadians later depict

---

[97] Her title as Lady of the Mountain is mysterious as Sumer did not have mountains. However, if she is descended from Ubaidians lore, then the mountain could be the Anatole Mountains of southern Turkey from which the Ubaidians probably came.

[98] Wilson, Before the Flood, Chapter 15, Empire of the Goddess

goddesses as mean-spirited and ferocious when they did not get their way, another form of anthropomorphism in a male- dominated society.

Inanna, called *Ishtar* by the Akkadians, was the goddess of sex, love, fertility and warfare, who in early Sumer was called the *lady of the sky*. Ishtar's cult lasted well into Biblical times although her name is not specifically mentioned.[99] Most city-states had fertility rite temples with a harem of priestesses who many times were just temple prostitutes legitimizing the most ancient profession. Many important people in antiquity were born from these temple prostitutes such as Sargon the Great of Akkad. Those born of a temple priestess without a known father were not considered illegitimate, nor did it give them less important status in society.

The Mesopotamians, like most other ancient cultures, created and worshiped gods identified with the forces of nature around them. Astrolatry is the association of deities with heavenly bodies such as the sun and the moon. The Sumerians had a moon-god *Nanna*, who the Semites of Abraham's time calls *Sin*, who was born of *Enlil*, the air-god, and his wife *Ninlil*, the air-goddess. Nanna, the moon-god, and his wife Ningal are the parents of *Utu*, the sun-god – "who rises in the mountain of the east and sets in the mountain of the west."[100] Utu is also the god of justice and law and is called Lord of truth. He is the brother of *Ishkur* and the twins *Inanna* and *Ereshkigal,* about whom we will learn more in Chapter 6 when we examine the *Netherworld*. Note that the moon god is the major astronomical deity in Sumerian lore rather than the sun. This is most likely because the moon had many divergent movements while the sun did the same thing every day. For instance, one of their poems states:

> "The moon-god Nanna travels across heavens bringing light to the pitch-dark lapis lazuli sky. The 'little ones', the stars, are scattered about him like grain while the 'big ones' (perhaps the planets) walk about him like wild oxen."[101]

---

[99] Jeremiah admonishes the Hebrews in several places about serving the "Queen of Heaven". Jer 7:18-20, Jer 41:17-19, Jer 44:25.

[100] *Sumerian Mythology*, Samuel Noah Kramer (University of Pennsylvania Press, Philadelphia, 1961), Organization of the Universe, pg. 41

[101] Ibid

When it came to the organization of the earth by the gods:

> "***Enlil,*** the air-god, caused the good day to come forth, set his mind to bring forth seed from the earth and to establish plenty, abundance and prosperity in the land."[102]

Enlil appointed ***Enten***, the farmer-god as his field worker. It was the water-god ***Enki,*** whose mother was ***Nammu,*** who begot ***Uttu***, the goddess of plants. Enki is very important as an organizer of ancient Sumer city-states. Both Enlil and Enki send ***Lahar,*** the cattle god, and ***Ashnan,*** the grain goddess, from heaven to earth to make abundant its cattle and grain. Their myths and poems brag how Enlil gave mankind the great inventions of their time such as the pickax and ox-driven plow, which made Sumer the first great agricultural society.[103] The worship of gods identified with nature is similar to, but not the same as the secular Pantheists of today. Pantheism is a form of atheism as it denies a superior creating deity, leaving the earth/cosmos itself as god with man being a physical part of that deity.[104] The Mesopotamians were polytheists, but they were clearly not atheists. There is an interesting prayer in the *Program of the Pageant of the Statue of the god Anu at Uruk*.[105] It calls on the many gods to bless Anu and gives us an idea of how they expressed their devotion to deity:

> "Great Anu, May heaven and earth bless you! May the deities Enlil, Ea, and Beletile bless you joyfully! May both the gods Sin and Shamash bless you when you appear! May the deities Nergal and Siba bless you with firm hearts! May the Igigi gods of heaven and the Anunnaki gods of earth bless you! May the god of the deep and the gods of

---

[102] Ibid, pg. 42

[103] Ibid, pg. 41-42

[104] Pantheism is defined as "the doctrine that God is the transcendent reality of which the material universe and human beings are only manifestations: it involves a denial of God's personality and expresses a tendency to identify God and nature; any religious belief or philosophical doctrine that identifies God with the Universe." Dictionary.com

[105] Pritchard, pg. 342. These incantations remind us of the Litany of the Saints in the Catholic Church.

> the Holy Shrine bless you! May they bless you daily every
> day, month and year!"

Mesopotamia was a god driven society. Everything that was good was from the gods, and most bad things were because man had displeased the gods – a unique form of morality. If the result of their petitions and offerings to the gods was not what the priests expected, they would sometimes make a civil leader or group of people scapegoats for having offended the gods in a past action. If a particular god was consistently unproductive, they would simply write him out of the pantheon or have him killed by a new god in a new great epic.

Each city-state had a god assigned to it from creation by the assembly of gods that established an order within the local pantheon.[106] Order did not mean peace as epics depict gods and even assemblies *of gods* that argued, quarreled and even killed each other over how to rule. A city-state's assigned god had the responsibility to protect and make prosperous its protectorate. When one city-state defeated another in war, their god many times became primary; and the loser's god faded away. Some of the ancient gods such as Anu, Enlil and Enki, which even after their cities' defeat, retained position of respect due to their ancient positions in the pantheon.

As the city-states became empires, new and fewer gods' assumed great power and prestige. Shortly after Abraham left Mesopotamia for Canaan, the Amorites established the city-state of Babylon, and Hammurabi declared **Marduk** its primary god.[107] As Babylon became a great power in the Near East for over a millennium, *Marduk* assumed the title of the chief deity of the empire and became most prominent and recognized in Mesopotamia and Canaan for hundreds of years. This was a step towards a universal god as opposed to many local deities and led to monolatry in Mesopotamia. Because of this godly protection, if anyone challenged the city or empire deity, it was considered an insult to the city or the state itself which became a political act equal to treason. This will not be the last time in history temple worship will be used as a political pawn. The Romans also worshiped a pantheon of gods. When Christians refused to make

---

[106] See chapter 9, *The gods of Canaan* for more information on the assembly of gods.

[107] The Amorite dynasty of Babylon was established in 1894 BC. Hammurabi, king of Babylon, ruled from 1795-1750 BC (Ancient History Encyclopedia)

their required annual offerings to the Roman gods, they were persecuted for treason, not for being Christian. Later Emperors will persecute them for professing and living the Christian life.

We find no evidence of a particular creed in the ancient Near Eastern beliefs although within the rituals we find rigid and dogmatic practices. Sumer had what they called "*me's* or divine laws, rules and regulations which they felt governed the universe from the days of its creation and kept it operating."[108] It seems clear by the poems depicting these "*me's*" that there were unacceptable human practices that displeased the gods. In their view, man would be punished if the gods were displeased; therefore, the emphasis within society was to make sure the gods were not unhappy with human activity. The will of the gods forced a human morality although we find little to indicate a written moral code showing how man is to relate to his fellow man as we will find later in the Torah given to the Jews by Moses.

The Mesopotamians also believed in demons that were seldom gods but rather spiritual beings that beguiled the gods and mankind causing sickness, disease, bad weather and even bad luck. Mark Smith in his book *The Origins of Biblical Monotheism* points out that in the Ugaritic Epic, "The Ba'al Cycle,"[109] the gods had homes in local mountains known to the people; but the demons were from far away mysterious places like the netherworld.[110] Smith points out that benevolent deity are often rendered anthropomorphic, whereas destructive divinities appear as monstrous in character. The benevolent deities were associated with domesticated animals such as the bull, calf, bird and cow; while the destructive deities were usually depicted by undomesticated animals emblematic of monsters such as snakes, serpents and multi-headed dragons. This concept was incorporated into the Hebrew scriptures where Satan is depicted as a serpent and the seven-headed dragon in Psalm 74:13-14; Job 26:13 and again in the New Testament in Revelation 12:3 and 13:1.[111] They used

---

[108] Kramer/History, pg. 95

[109] See chapter nine, Gods of Canaan

[110] Mark S Smith, *Origins of Biblical Monotheism*, Israel's Polytheistic Background and the Ugaritic Texts (Oxford University Press, New York, 2001) pg. 28-30) (hereafter Smith/Origins)

[111] Ibid, pg. 32-33

priestly-class exorcists to rid people of the demons that possessed them, which is a religious belief that remains with us today in Christianity. As we shall see below, these demons prowled the *Netherworld*.

Astrology was a way for the gods to transmit the future fate of people. For this reason, the movement of the heavenly bodies was studied extensively in the temple observatories which by the time of Abraham were the high-rise Ziggurat Temples. The gods also used *divination* to help control the environment. This divination sometimes came in "dreams, visions or other supernatural interventions"[112] where the gods would foretell the future or warn of disaster. So, when God appeared to Abraham in a dream or vision, the occurrence would not have seemed out of place in his society when he related the contents of the message to Terah or his friends.

This polytheistic form of religion made for a relatively peaceful civilization at a time when other world cultures were still nomads constantly at war. We see the civilized culture in the Sumerians in their written abhorrence to the barbarity of the Gutians. It was in this world that Terah and his family lived; therefore it should not surprise us that **Terah served other gods**. We can assume that his family did the same.

There were good gods and bad gods much like the Judeo/Christian concept of good and bad angels. The Mesopotamian deities are quite similar to our Christian concept of angels in that they have specific chores to do for other gods, or for man, as Gabriel, Michael and Raphael do for God the Father. There are also many monstrous creatures and demons that are sometimes subservient or threatening to the gods. The ancients acted out their fears and had vivid imaginations. The seven-headed serpent/dragon in the epic *Gilgamesh and land of the living* may be prophetic to a very familiar story in Revelation that tells us:

> **Then another sign appeared in the sky; it was a huge red dragon with seven heads and ten horns, and on its heads were seven diadems.[113]**

---

[112] *Everyday Life in Ancient Mesopotamia*, Jean Bottero (John Hopkins Univ. Press, Baltimore, 1992), pg. 187-188, *A Long Tradition of Divinatory Schools*

[113] Rev 12:3

There does not seem to be reference to a universal creating deity in any of the ancient Near East pantheons. Every society had its own creating god or goddess, and some claimed an assembly of gods. Some of these begat other gods, some create various matter, and some create men. The concept of a universal creating deity will not come to mankind until Abraham's descendant Moses is exposed to the true God of creation on Mount Sinai. It is essential to our story of the Hebrew's quest for monotheism to understand that civilized man's concept of deity at the time of Abraham was far from what we know it to be today. The idea of only one God would have been an anathema and even heretical concept to man at this time in history. To me, this fact makes God's call to Abraham a truly momentous event in the history of mankind.

In the Sumerian Creation story *Atra-khasis*, mankind had not yet been created; therefore, the gods had to perform all the hard labor of farming, digging canals and fishing the rivers for food. In the world's first recorded labor dispute, the gods threatened violence due to the stress of work:

> "Every single one of the gods has declared war; … Excessive toil has killed us, our work was heavy, the distress much." [114]

The god Enki came to the rescue in the Epic *Enki, Ninmakh, and the Creation of Mankind* when he created man out of clay in the same way that he too was created by the god Apsu's *fathering clay*. It seems it was also a virgin birth:

> "And when, without any male, you have built it up in it, may you give birth to humankind! Without the sperm of a male, she gave birth to offspring to the embryo of humankind." [115]

Enki created man to serve the gods so man could do all the hard work. Man would later do the same thing when he created the abomination of slavery. As man was lower in the hierarchy of beings, when the gods were unhappy with men, man suffered. Therefore, man's sin caused a rift with

---

[114] Arnold/Beyer, Epic of Atra-khasis, pg. 24

[115] Ibid, pg. 21

the gods – a guilt that would carry into Jewish and Christian tradition. That the gods rebelled because they no longer wanted to work brings to mind the Latin term *Non Serviam* which means *I will not serve* and is attributed to Satan when he refused to serve God any longer.

Temple Sacrifice

The ancient pagans appeased their gods by making available each god's presumed needs in temple offerings and sacrifices in the form of what humans would want and need, Anthropotheism. These sacrifices were offered in temples, later called Ziggurats, controlled by a priestly class of men and women who became as politically powerful as the monarch in their society. This practice will continue with the Hebrews but with only a male priesthood. Any rift with the gods could be eliminated if man made the proper sacrifice on the altar of the Temple. In the second book of Samuel, King David's sin of imposing a census tax on all the people was punished by God, who through the prophet Gad gave David a choice of three alternatives of disaster upon the people of David's kingdom. David chose three days of pestilence. The prophet Gad told David that God could be appeased and stop the pestilence if David built an altar and offer holocausts and peace offerings. When David did so, the pestilence ceased.[116] The God of Israel, like the gods of Sumer and Akkad, will severely punish not only the sinner, but all of Israel when David strayed from His commands, even threatening to kill them all.[117] The sacrificial system of worshiping God was codified in Judaism when Moses instructed the Hebrews in the theology of Temple Sacrifice extensively in Leviticus. The recorded history of man from the time of polytheism in ancient Mesopotamia through the Temple period in Judaism included this form of appeasing man's gods in Temples with very explicit rituals for sacrifice. While this practice seems strange and even pagan to us today, it was the way of life in the second Millennium BC.

---

[116] 2 Sam 24:1-25

[117] This idea of the sins of others being laid onto future generations is foreign to Christians today. The Catholic Church teaches that "Sin is a personal act." (ccc 1866)

In the eyes of the ancient Mesopotamian, man's whole purpose in life was to please the gods; therefore, prayer and sacrifice to the gods were a crucial part of their birth, marriage and burial rites. Everyone from the peasant to the king made pilgrimages to the temple to give homage to the gods. As we can see below, the gods were very well fed. The food was put before the statue of the god in the temple accompanied by music and incense. Below is a list of items put before the god Anu at Uruk (Ereck):

> "12 vessels of wine, 2 vessels of milk, 108 vessels of various beers, 243 loaves of bread, 29 bushels of dates, 21 rams, 2 bulls, a bullock, 8 lambs, 60 birds, 3 cranes, 7 ducks, 4 wild boars, 3 ostrich eggs, 3 duck eggs"[118]

Everett Ferguson in his book *Backgrounds to Early Christianity* explains that these ancient religious sacrifices were used to unify the people within the community and emphasized the religious rite:

> "To the ancients the essence of religion was the rite, which was thought of as a process for securing and maintaining correct relations with the world of uncharted forces around man, and the myth, which gave the traditional reason for the rite and the traditional (but changing) view of those forces."[119]

Human Sacrifice

While human sacrifice was not common in the temple worship, it evidently had a role in the burial rite of some of the kings of ancient Sumer. Sir Leonard Woolley, an English archaeologist who made the first major excavation of the ancient city state of Ur in 1927, found a *death pit* or cemetery of kings from 3500 BC up the Third Dynasty of Ur in 2000

---

[118] Pritchard, "Daily sacrifices to the gods of the city of Uruk", pg. 343)

[119] Everett Ferguson, *Backgrounds of Early Christianity* (Michigan: William B. Eerdmans Publishing Company, Third ed. 2003), pg. 150

BC, which was the time when Abraham lived there.[120] These burial sites included the remains of attendants buried in layers above the king quite similar to those in Egypt. Several gold cups were found next to an attendant or queen who most scholars believe held the poison that was voluntarily taken by the victim. There were also signs of blunt force trauma to some of the victims buried with the king indicating that not all volunteered for this ordeal. The final layer of the grave included the body of an important person such as the queen or governor and then a grave marker to identify the king. This is the only site discovered so far that indicates that kings of ancient Sumer were buried in the similar manner to the Egyptians that we see memorialized in a later era. The voluntary human sacrifices, which could only benefit the king or king/god, are examples of how serious the citizens of this age took their responsibility to serve the gods. There is, however, a question whether these burials were the exception or the rule in Mesopotamia, as the kings who were buried in this cemetery were not listed on the king lists extant in the writings of ancient Sumer. For this reason, there is no consensus of Sumerian scholars that all kings were buried this way.

The subject of human sacrifice brings us to the question of why Abraham was willing to sacrifice his only son Isaac at the request of God.[121] At the time that Abraham left Ur, some forms of human sacrifice were practiced.[122] In Chapter 2 of Leviticus, Moses admonishes the Hebrews that they are not to sacrifice their children to the Molech, the Canaanite god of fire[123] and, again in Deuteronomy calling it an abomination when the Canaanites burn their sons and daughters to their gods.[124] The king of Moab, who was losing a battle with the Israelites at the time, had no problem sacrificing his own son:

---

[120] Leonard Woolley, *Excavations at Ur – A record of the twelve- year work* (Google books, 2009), Hereafter Woolley, Excavations.

[121] Gen 22:1-19

[122] The Carthaginians of north-east Africa, who were eventually destroyed by the Romans, were also Semites. Archeologists have found evidence of child sacrifice similar to what was found in Canaan in the remains of Carthage.

[123] Gen 20:2

[124] Dt 12:31

> *So he took his firstborn, who was to succeed him, and*
> *offered him as a burnt offering upon the wall.*[125]

We see how serious the Hebrews considered human sacrifice hundreds of years after Abraham in Chapter 11 of the Book of Judges. Jephthah, the son of Gilead, made a vow that if he is successful in his war with the Ammonites, he would offer as a holocaust the first person he sees coming out of his door after he is victorious. To his horror, it is his only daughter. After giving her *two months to mourn her virginity with her companions* he offered her up as promised.[126] This practice did not end easily as we see as late as king Josiah of Judah (641-609 BC), after reading the words of the law that he found in the temple:

> *The King also defiled Topheth in the Valley of*
> *Ben-hinnom, so that there would no longer be any*
> *immolation of sons or daughter by fire in honor of*
> *Molech.*[127]

Hebrew Scriptures make it clear that a Semite from the Third Dynasty of Ur, living in Canaan in 2000 BC, would not find the request to sacrifice his son to a god that unusual. We remember from Genesis that when Abraham was about to fulfill the request of God and sacrifice his son, God delivered a scapegoat in the form of a ram caught in the thickets to sacrifice in lieu of his son Isaac:

> *Abraham looked up and saw a single ram caught by*
> *its horns in the thicket. So Abraham went and took*
> *the ram and offered it up as a burnt offering in place*
> *of his son.*[128]

A ram caught by its horns in a thicket is a vivid description of the scene. But, was this description just to paint a picture for the reader or did it have other significance to Abraham? Leonard Woolley in his excavations of the

---

[125] II Kings 3:27
[126] Jugs 11:37-39
[127] II Kgs 23:10
[128] Gen 22:13

death pit in Ur found two very interesting statues in separate graves at the site. They are the figure of a golden goat with his head entangled in what looks like the limbs of a tree or thicket. The statue below was found buried in a grave of a king that lived less than a hundred years before Abraham left Ur. The fact that these statues were found in two separate graves that had human sacrifice would make us think that the figure had some significance to either sacrificial death or some other religious rite. Was this a religious symbol that becomes the basis for the ram in the thicket story in Genesis? More than one archeologist and biblical scholar has made this connection since this incredible discovery.

We cannot leave the subject of Temple Sacrifice without wondering how man's sacrificial offering of physical things to gods, and even the one God of the Hebrews, assists God's Plan of Salvation. Yet, the Holy Spirit led Moses to clearly instruct the Jews in the sacrificial rite listing specific offerings for specific faults of man. As important as Temple Sacrifice was to the Jews before the temple in Jerusalem was destroyed by the Romans

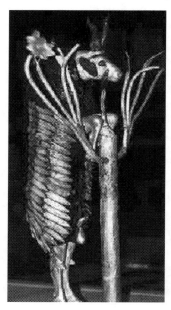

in 70 AD, it is difficult to understand how Judaism simply abandoned Temple Sacrifice. God's own son Jesus, as a practicing Jew, will perform the Pascal Sacrifice rite at the Last Supper, which included offerings of unleavened bread and wine reminiscent of Melchizedek. Further, we Christians believe that Jesus' sacrifice of His own life on the cross was necessary to free all mankind from the *Original Sin* of our First Parents. Looking back over man's history of Temple Sacrifice, we can see that God was preparing His people to understand the ultimate sacrifice – the sacrifice of God's own Son to God the Father. Only this sacrifice would be sufficient. After the *Crucifixion,* Judaism is no longer a sacrificial religion.

CHAPTER FIVE

GENESIS-LIKE STORIES IN ANCIENT MESOPOTAMIA

The mystery of the Kingdom of God has been granted to you. But to those outside everything comes in parables. Jesus to his Apostles explaining the parable of the Sower[129]

The Gospels of the New Testament are ripe with parables wherein Jesus used old familiar tales to impart theological lessons. It can be said that Moses, through the Holy Spirit, did the same in the Torah when he used old familiar Semitic tales from Mesopotamia to impart theological lessons.

Now it is time to examine the ancient myths and epics of Sumer and Akkad that are similar to those found in the Hebrew Scriptures. The similarities of these ancient stories to those in Geneses are what drove the biblical scholars of the nineteenth and twentieth centuries to rediscover and analyze the ancient Near Eastern texts. Thanks to the fact that the Sumerians and Akkadians used the cuneiform system of writing on fire-hardened clay tablets, their stories have survived over five thousand years. Many of these stories are fully or partially extant today. The efforts of archeologists, literary scholars and theologians have made the stories of ancient Mesopotamia come alive for us. Each find takes us back even further in time than we thought that man had established civilized society. As we shall see in the *deluge* story, incredible finds that are only now

---

[129] Mk 4: 11

available as a result of advanced technology are giving us a more clear understanding that perhaps many of the stories of the Hebrew Scriptures are more historical than was originally thought.

A Momentous Discovery

It is informative to learn how biblical scholars first became interested in the secular history of Abraham's time and how it changed our understanding of the Hebrew Scriptures. There were important men in antiquity that have helped us understand our past, and Scripture identifies one of those men:

> *And the other peoples whom the great and illustrious Assurbanipal[130] transported and settled in the city of Samaria and elsewhere in the province West-of-Euphrates, as follows ...* [131]

This reference to the movement of the Persians from Susa and Elam into Samaria in the northern kingdom of Israel is the only place in the Bible where we find Assurbanipal, the history-loving king of Assyria who ruled from 668 to 629 BC. This event in itself was of grave importance to the history of the Jews as it eventually defined the Samaritan people of the northern kingdom of Israel that became an anathema to the Jews of Jesus' time.

More important to our story is that this same Assurbanipal was a great student of ancient Akkadian and Sumerian literature and founded a library in his capital city of Nineveh, placing in it over 10,000 different ancient texts. To date, Assyriolosists have documented over 30,000 clay tablets from this site. We have extant a letter where Assurbanipal instructed an officer named Shandanu to copy and collect from his extended empire any tablet or ritualistic text and to bring it to his palace. The library includes texts of history, genealogy, law, medicine, mathematics, astronomy, poetry

---

[130] Assurbanipal is also spelled Ashurbanipal or Ashshurbanipal. He was an Assyrian king, the son of Esarhaddon and the last strong king of the Neo-Assyrian Empire. (685 BC-627 BC) Wikipedia

[131] Ezra 4:10 (NABRE) actually says illustrious Osnappar but footnotes say is probably Assurbanipal.

and prose.[132] Assurbanipal copied ancient texts from Sumer and Akkad, most of which have since disappeared because of their age, leaving only small fragments of the original texts in Sumer. It is his copies of the ancient works that have given us the complete stories of the great literature of the third millennium BC that we will discover later in this work. When Nineveh was destroyed in 612 BC, Assurbanipal's palace, which contained the thousands of tablets, parchments and papyri, was burned to the ground much like the great library of Alexandria later in history. While the parchments and papyri were destroyed, the fire hardened the clay tablets, which survived. They were re-discovered in 1853 by Hormuzd Rassam, an assistant to the English Assyriolosists Austen Layard and Henry Rawlinson. Many of the tablets, which were written in the cuneiform language (which Rawlinson had just recently helped to translate) were returned to England and stored in the British Museum where they sat for almost twenty years with little attention paid to them.

One day in 1872, a self-taught Assyriologist named George Smith was translating tablet XI and was shocked to find the lines that read:

> "The seventh day when it came, I brought out a dove, I let it loose, off went the dove but then it returned, there was no place to land, so back it came to me … I brought out a raven, I let it loose, off went the raven, it saw the waters receding, finding food, bowing and bobbing, it did not come back to me."

Being a student of the Bible, Smith knew he had seen this story before and immediately went to the book of Genesis where he read:

> *At the end of forty days, Noah opened the hatch of the arc he had made, and he released a raven. It flew back and forth until the waters dried off from the earth. Then he released a dove, to see if the waters had lessened on the earth.[133]*

---

[132] Ian Wilson, *Before the Flood* (St. Martin's Press, 2005) pg. 251 (hereafter Wilson)
[133] Gen 8:6-8

Smith was amazed as he knew that Genesis was supposed to have been written by Moses, who died in either fourteenth or twelfth century BC.[134] How did this Noah-like flood story end up in a piece of literature that Smith and his colleagues had proven to be thousands of years older than the Exodus? When he made his discovery known to the London Society of Biblical Archaeology, it was an immediate sensation, and there was a clamor for more information from these strange clay tablets gathering dust in the British Museum. This led to Smith and others making additional trips to Nineveh where they found even older literary works, including creation stories and stories of heaven and hell. All of these writings were from the ancient polytheistic religions of Mesopotamia leading Biblical scholars to realize that much of our Judeo/Christian theology may have come to us from a pagan society thousands of years before God revealed Himself to Abraham. These discoveries shook the complacency and certitude of the theologians of their day, and Bible study would never be the same. What George Smith had discovered on tablet XI were the last few lines of the great Sumerian *Epic of Gilgamesh* depicting the Deluge. This Epic, which came to be known as the world's first great work of literature, included a Noah-like flood story incredibly similar to Genesis. Since that time this same *Epic of Gilgamesh* has been found in almost every ancient society including Hittite and Canaanite literature. Obviously this was a classic piece of literature in its day.[135]

Smith's discovery began a concerted scientific study of Sacred Scripture. There was a flood of serious biblical scholars who wanted to know what secular history could reveal about the stories in the Bible. The more the science of archaeology and linguistic studies improved in the nineteenth century, the more ancient writing became available which directed scholars to other locations revealing even more discoveries. We are only beginning to discover our past. As it is doing with increasing frequency, science is inadvertently giving an historical basis to much of Sacred Scripture. Interestingly enough, this was a time in history when the thinkers of the

---

[134] There is quite a dispute as to when the Hebrews exited Egypt in the Exodus. We make a detailed analysis of this dispute in Chapter 11, "After Abraham".

[135] N.K. Sandars, *The Epic of Gilgamesh, an English version with an introductory* (England, Penguin Books, 1972)

recently avowed *age of enlightenment*[136] were telling folks that scripture was nothing more than fables. But as we shall see, this was just the beginning of a new look into ancient scripture.

The Creation Story

The *First Story of Creation* found in chapter 1 of Genesis gives us the familiar and poetic seven days of creation by God. This masterpiece of literature does not seem to be repeated in ancient lore, but there is one paragraph in the ancient Sumerian epic *The Deluge* reminiscent of the linear *week of creation* in Genesis. It refers to the pantheon of gods as creators rather than God the Father, and the order is different, but sounds familiar:

> "After Anu, Enlil, Enki and Ninhursag had fashioned the black-headed people (the Sumerians), vegetation luxuriated from the earth, animals, and four-legged creatures of the plain were brought artfully into existence---.*"[137]*

Within the ancient Mesopotamian myths there was no consistent creation story, but rather several different versions where the numerous gods were created from a begetter and his consort out of a chaos of nothingness. Interestingly enough, the Hebrew Scriptures also has more than one story of creation. In chapter 2 of Genesis we find the *Second Story of Creation*.[138] While the first *Story of Creation* may not have a counterpart within Mesopotamian epics, the *Second Story of Creation* in Genesis could well been inspired by the *Epic of Atra-Khasis,* where the god Enki creates man from clay. Genesis 2 begins describing a barren earth:

... ... there was no field shrub on earth and no grass of the fields had sprouted, for the Lord God had sent no

---

[136] *Age of Enlightenment*: An intellectual and scientific movement in the 18th century Europe which was characterized by a rational and scientific approach to religious, social, political, and economic issues. Dictionary.com

[137] Pritchard, The Deluge, pg. 43

[138] Gen 1 is thought to be from the P (Priestly) source; and Gen 2 from the J (Yahweh) source. Friedman, The Bible, Sources revealed, pg. 33,35

> *rain upon the earth and there was no man to till the*
> *soil. But a stream was welling up out of the earth and*
> *was watering all the surface of the ground. The Lord*
> *God formed man out of the clay of the ground and blew*
> *into his nostrils the breath of life, and man became a*
> *living being.*

The Sumerian god Enki is the god of fresh water and is depicted in reliefs found on temple walls with water flowing up from the ground. In the *Epic Atra-Khasis*, we find Enki creating man from clay in a similar manner after the gods had rebelled over all the work they had to endure on earth:

> "From his flesh and blood, let Nintu (Enki's assistant)
> mix clay, that god and man may be thoroughly mixed in
> the clay, let there be a spirit from the god's flesh so that
> we may hear the drum for the rest of time. Let it proclaim
> living man as its sign, so that this is not forgotten let there
> be a spirit."[139]

In the Epic of Atra-Khasis, the gods created man so the gods would no longer have to toil on the earth. The Mesopotamian gods created man for the purpose of providing them with food, drink and shelter as we have seen when we discussed *Temple Sacrifices*. Man purpose in life was to be the gods' servants.[140] Genesis 2 may be referring to a similar work related situation where is says: "*there was no man to till the soil*," which would imply that up until that time someone else was tilling the soil.

The Creation Epic of Akkad known as *Enuma Elish*[141] is the most complete creation story that we have found to date, and it gives us great insight

---

[139] Arnold/Beyer, Epic of Atra-Khasis, pg. 24, this quote is also reminiscent of God placing a soul into man. We will further discuss this issue in chapter 6, *Life after Death*.

[140] Kramer/History pg. 101

[141] Enuma Elish was the first two words in the epic. Many epic stories are identified this way.

into the Mesopotamian concept of deity.[142] This story tells of the ancient struggle between cosmic order and chaos. This itself is quite interesting as scientists today are toying with a *Chaos Theory* to explain the existence of the universe.[143] This epic was of such importance to the theology of the time that it was recited by the scribes for all to hear at the beginning of each year, much as the Hebrews did with the Torah years later.

There are similarities in the beginning of the Creation Epic and the first chapter of Genesis where God created all things. In the Creation Epic it is a *begetter* and his *consort* who bring forth all there is. Here are a few lines from the story:

> "When on high the heaven had not been named, Firm ground below had not been called by name, naught but primordial Apsu, their begetter and Mummu-Tiamat, she who bore them all, their waters commingling as a single body; ... ... When no gods whatever had been brought into being, uncalled by name, their destinies undetermined --- Then it was that the gods were formed within them. Anu begot in his image Nudimmud."[144]

Apsu, the male spirit of life-giving fresh water and the abyss, is called the begetter, and ***Tiamat***, the female spirit of salt water and chaos, is his consort; they commingled to form all the gods. The gods later bring forth man. Genesis mimics the creation epics in that God made matter out of nothing – a creating God. The polytheistic version is devoid of a single

---

[142] This epic included Marduk, the primary god of Babylon, which was established after Abraham left Ur III for Canaan; therefore, this story would not have been one he would have been familiar. However, as it is quite similar to ancient Sumerian stories, it is probably based on Sumerian legends.

[143] Chaos theory: *"A field of study in mathematics, with applications in several disciplines including meteorology, physics, engineering, economics and biology. Chaos theory studies the behavior of dynamical systems that are highly sensitive to initial conditions, an effect which is popularly referred to as the butterfly effect."* Kellert, Stephen H. *"In the Wake of Chaos: Unpredictable Order in Dynamical Systems"*. (Chicago, University of Chicago Press. p. 32)

[144] Pritchard, *The Creation Epic*, pg. 61

creator so they manufactured a human understanding of this mystery to bring about matter from nothingness. Much like the scientists of today, who are stuck in their *Big Bang Theory*[145] with the question, "who made the thing that banged?" *the* ancients acknowledged a begetter and consort, but do not tell us from where they came.

Like God in Genesis, who decided to destroy evil man with the flood, so do Apsu and Tiamat. After they had created the gods, they decided to kill off the first bunch and start all over. Their excuse was that the gods were a noisy bunch and therefore needed to be destroyed:

> "Apsu, opening his mouth, said unto resplendent Tiamat: "Their ways are verily loathsome unto me. By day I find no relief, nor repose by night. I will destroy, I will wreck their ways that quiet may be restored. Let us have our rest."[146]

It seems that the god *Ea* (Enki in Sumer), the good father-god of the hero-god *Marduk* in the epic, was wise to their plans and was able to stop the slaughter of the gods:

> "Surpassing in wisdom, accomplished, resourceful … The all wise, saw through their scheme." He then sought out Apsu, and poured sleep upon him. And while he was powerless: He loosened his band, tore off his tiara, removed his halo[147] and put it on himself. Having fettered Apsu, he slew him"[148]

---

[145] *Big Bang Theory*: a theory that deduces a cataclysmic birth of the universe (big bang) from the observed expansion of the universe, cosmic background radiation, abundance of the elements, and the laws of physics. Dictionary.com

[146] Pritchard, Ibid

[147] The gods have halos throughout these stories and all seem to have messengers which the Hebrews called angels. These similarities are too frequent to not have some connection.

[148] Ibid

There was to be a great battle in the heavens between the good gods and the evil gods. It will be Marduk, who will battle Tiamat and the turncoat evil gods that joined her. He will finally kill her, she who begat them all. It reminds us of the great battle in heaven between the Archangel Michael and Satan and his minions in the book of Revelation. After this turmoil, the gods created the cosmos from the remains of Tiamat with part of her being the land, and part of her being the heavens. The story also includes a reference of darkness turned to light; then the gods determined the years, the months, and the days much as God the Father does in Chapter 1 of Genesis. The main difference in the order of creation is that in the ancient Mesopotamian creation stories the gods were first created, and then they created man. In many ways the gods of ancient Mesopotamia were similar to the Judeo/Christian concept of angels as they are situated in the grand hierarchy of creation between the creator and man. In our story we see the god Marduk create man from the blood of Tiamat:

> "Blood I will mass and cause bones to be. I will establish a savage, man shall be his name. Verily, savage-man I will create. He shall be charged with the service of the gods that they might be at ease."[149]

The idea of man being originally a savage is quite interesting. Those who adhere to the secular theory of evolution also see man as originally a savage who evolves into the *Homo sapiens* that we are today. We also find in the great Epic *of Gilgamesh*, Gilgamesh's companion Enkidu, a wild beast formed from clay and saliva by **Aruru,** the goddess of creation.[150] He was turned into a man after bedding with Shamhat a prostitute provided by Gilgamesh. These ancient stories of man's creation quite frequently involve clay or dirt. We wonder if this concept influenced the authors of Genesis, which states that God created man from the dust of the earth.

It is also interesting that there are places in Genesis where God is sometimes in the plural,[151] which we Christians see as a prophetic reference to the Trinity. Possibly this was a typo by a scribe somewhere along the way in

[149] Pritchard, Creation Epic, Tablet VI, pg. 68

[150] Here again we see a goddess as a creator in early Sumer. This Epic was written as far back as 2500 BC.

[151] Gen 6:2 "the sons of God"

history. It is also possible that the author of Genesis used these ancient creation stories as a reference where God is depicted as gods throughout these epics.

The Paradise Lost Story

The Sumerians also had a paradise myth, like Eden, which fortunately is nearly extant. The land in question (sometimes called a city) is *Dilmun* which according to the poem is a place that is pure, clean, and bright. It is a land where there is neither sickness nor death as:

> "The land Dilmun is pure, the Dilmun is clean ---- the land Dilmun is most bright. ---- in Dilmun the raven utters no cries, the lion kills not, the wolf snatches not the lamb, ---- The sick-eyed says not 'I am sick-eyed, the old women says not I am an old woman, the old man says not 'I am an old man' "[152]

There was one minor problem: they had a fresh water shortage so they called on the great water-god Enki, who ordered Utu the sun-god to bring fresh water for the plants to flourish. Enki brings up fresh water from the earth much we observed earlier in chapter 1 of Genesis:

> **But a stream was welling up out of the earth and watering the surface of the ground.**[153]

It was this fresh water that made Dilmun into the garden paradise where **Ninhursag**, the great mother-goddess, grew eight plants that were somehow mysterious and forbidden to eat. It was the forbidden nature of the plants that caused Enki to have one of his minion gods pick the eight plants so he could eat them *to know their heart*. In the Garden of Eden, did Satan not say that the forbidden fruit would do a similar thing?

---

[152] Pritchard, *Enki and Ninhursag: a Paradise Myth*, pg. 38
[153] Gen 2:6

It is only about the fruit of the tree in the middle of the garden that God said, "You shall not eat it or even touch it, or else you will die."[154]

Ninhursag discovers Enki's trespass and claims that due to this sin, until he dies, she will not look upon him with the *eye of life*. The peace of Dilmun will change. Enki started to have pains in eight organs of his body – to match the eight plants he consumed and was about to die when Enlil, the king of the gods convinces Ninhursag to remove the curse on Enki. She relents, but enacts her revenge when she asks Enki:

"My brother, what hurts thee? My jaw hurts me – my mouth hurts me – my arm hurts me – my rib hurts me"[155]

After this, Dilmun is no longer free of pain and even the goddesses now suffer childbirth pains as also happened to Eve's descendants in Genesis (man is not in this epic). There is also a very interesting theory by Samuel Kramer about that rib that hurt Enki in Dilmun. Let us look at what he wrote:

"The Sumerian word for rib is "ti" (pronounced tee). The goddess created for the healing of Enki's rib is called Nin-ti, 'the lady of the rib'. But, the Sumerian word ti also means 'to make live'. The name Nin-ti therefore means 'the lady who makes live', as well as the lady of the rib. Eve, according to the Biblical notion means approximately 'she who makes live'"[156]

It is Kramer's opinion that this was the basis for the authors of Genesis choosing Adam's rib to make Eve. If he is right, the relationship of the paradise lost stories in Dilmun and Eden is quite likely. Dilmun has yet to be found by archeologists, but most ancient references would seem to place Dilmun on the Persian Gulf near the Bahrain of today. Some place it in southwest Iran. Both may be right as the Landsat space images of this area

---

[154] Gen 3:3

[155] Pritchard, *Enki and Ninhursag: a Paradise Myth*. Pg. 40

[156] Kramer/History, pg. 144

show that the whole top of the Persian Gulf of today was dry land before the de-glaciation of the last Ice Age. The satellite image also revealed the dry-bed remains of the Pison and Gihon rivers mentioned with the Tigris and Euphrates in Genesis as emptying into Eden.[157]

The Flood Story

The British linguist George Smith's discovery of a Noah-like flood story in the *Epic of Gilgamesh* caused quite a stir in academia. Notwithstanding the exaggerated adventures within the epic, Gilgamesh was a king of Uruk in about 2600 B.C. There have been numerous copies of this epic found in ancient Mesopotamia. University of Pennsylvania archeologists found similar tablets in the ancient Sumerian city of Nippur, with only a portion of the story legible, but in the Sumerian language, and obviously much older. It is clear from the many copies found throughout the ancient Near East that this was a classic piece of literature. We can assume that it was read and maybe even re-written as a school project by Abraham before he left Ur for Haran.

The Noah figure in the Sumerian version is *Ziusudra*, who is described in the texts as a pious, God-fearing king, constantly on the lookout for divine revelations in dreams and incantations.[158] First Ziusudra is instructed by a good god to stand by a wall and listen to the plan of the assembly of gods to destroy the earth. There are lines missing, and next we see the king in the Ark during the deluge:

> "Stand by the wall at my left side … By the wall I will say a word to thee, take my word, and give ear to my instructions. By our … A flood will sweep over the cult centers; to destroy the seed of mankind … … Is the decision, the word of the assembly of the gods?"
>
> "Then did Ziusudra, the king, the pasisu, of the … … build giant … All the windstorms, exceedingly powerful,

---

[157] Gen 2:10-14

[158] Pritchard, *The Deluge*, pg. 42. A footnote from Pritchard's translation notes that Ziusudra is among the king lists of Sumer and lived in the city Shuruppak.

> attacked as one, at the same time, for seven days and seven nights, the flood had swept over the land, and the huge boat had been tossed about by the windstorm on the great waters ... Ziusudra opened a window of the huge boat, ... The king kills an ox, slaughters a sheep ... then Ziusudra the king, the preserver of the name, of vegetation and of the seed of mankind ... In the land of crossing, the land of Dilmun, the place where the sun rises, they caused to dwell."[159]

Less than a third of this tablet is extant so there is much missing. It begins with the gods telling why they want to destroy the earth, and ends with the small amount of lines we have above. Clearly this story is a Noah-like flood story from ancient Sumer circa 2500 BC. The later versions found complete in the Assurbanipal library could well be the whole Sumerian version, or could be a later Akkadian version of the same story as Atra-hais was the name of the Noah-like person. Our story of discovery does not end here. In January of 2014, Dr. Irving Finkel, who like George Smith worked at the British Museum, published a new a book titled *The Ark before Noah*.[160] In his book he translates a small cuneiform tablet (small enough to fit into a man's hand) from 1850 to 1750 BC that fills in some of the missing details of the flood story we read above. This tablet was from the later Akkadian version of the flood and the Noah-like figure was Atra-hais.

---

[159] Ibid, pp. 42-44

[160] *The Ark Before the Noah, Decoding the Story of the Flood*. Irving Finkel, (Published by Hodder & Stoughton 2014). Dr.Irving Finkel is Assistant Keeper of Ancient Mesopotamian (i.e. Sumerian, Babylonian and Assyrian) script, languages and cultures Department: Middle East at the British Museum headquartered in London's Bloomsbury. He is the curator in charge of cuneiform inscriptions on tablets of clay from ancient Mesopotamia, of which the Middle East Department has the largest collection - some 130,000 pieces - of any modern museum. This work involves reading and translating all sorts of inscriptions, sometimes working on ancient archives to identify manuscripts that belong together, or even join to one another. https://www.hodder.co.uk/books/detail.page?isbn=9781444757071. This particular tablet was brought to Dr. Finkel on a museum open day by Douglas Simmons, whose father, Leonard, brought it back to England in a tea-chest full of curios, after wartime service in the Middle East with the RAF.

The tablet not only says "the animals are to enter the Ark by twos," but that the Ark was a round boat called a *Coracle* by the ancient and current boatman of the Tigris and Euphrates rivers. Noah's coracle Ark was to be 3,600 square meters or about two-thirds the size of soccer field made of reed rope wrapped around a wooden frame and sealed inside and out with two kinds of bitumen. The tablet even advised the exact amount of rope to be used.[161] We see clearly from these discoveries of ancient lore that a flood story like the one in Genesis was well known in the Semitic world more than a thousand years before Moses related them in the Hebrew Scriptures. Finkel's opinion is that the Jews discovered the story of the flood from these tablets when they were in the Babylonian captivity and brought them back to Judah where they were included in the Hebrew Scriptures. It seems to me that Abraham was the most likely source of the story of the flood as Moses would have had access to the patriarch's archives.

We find more than one story of the flood in ancient mythology including the lore of India, China, the Americas and even Australia. Whether it was a flood that covered the whole earth can be argued; however, most scholars believe that there was a cataclysmic flood event in early Mesopotamian history. From 1922 to 1935, the archeologist Sir Leonard Woolley excavated the city-state of Ur and found evidence of a major flood some time during the time of the Ubaidians around 5000 BC. He felt he had found proof of *Noah's Flood* but as we shall see, he was mistaken.[162]

A cataclysmic flood would not be unusual for a society built along two major rivers and the Persian Gulf. We must also consider the remnants of the last Ice Age which peaked about twenty thousand years ago and caused sea levels to recede as much as 400 feet. Scientists tell us that while the glaciers melted, the seas rose again in two or three major stages as there were a few *mini ice ages* along the way with the last one around 7600 BC. While the seas rose there had to be major flooding of low lands such as Sumer and Akkad. As the earth warmed (as much as 7 degrees F, climatologists tell us) there would have been considerable rainfall resulting from these warming times. We see the same extreme weather patterns today during our century long warming trend when the temperature of the southern

---

[161] http://www.theguardian.com/culture/2014/jan/24/babylonian-tablet-noah-ark-constructed-british-museum

[162] Woolley Excavations

and northern hemisphere oceans differ and then come together to cause major storm patterns.[163]

Most of the flood stories, other than the Semitic ones that are called *Noah-like stories*, were a result of rising waters as they tell of the *flood coming up* to them, which clearly refers to rising waters.[164] The Noah-like stories tell of a deluge from above and are clearly different. So, we are back to square one – or are we? In 1999, William Ryan, an oceanographer from Columbia University working in sea-level and sediment studies, and Walter Pitman, a specialist in plate tectonics, published an explosive book entitled *Noah's Flood, The New Scientific Discoveries about the Event that Changed History*[165] They developed *The Black Sea Burst-Through* theory which opines that in around 5600 BC there was a cataclysmic event at the narrow end of the

A Last glaciation

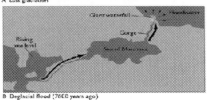

B Deglacial flood (7600 years ago)

Bosporus Strait that separated the salt waters of the Aegean Sea with a fresh water lake today known as the Black Sea. At that time the earthen land bridge that had separated the two bodies of water collapsed, causing the salt water of the Aegean to cascade down into the fresh waters of the Black Sea Lake, causing it to rise 300 feet.[166] Their book exhibits the two maps here that show the lowest sea level at the *last glaciation* and the *Deglacial flood of 7600 BC* with the eventual breakthrough in 5600 BC at the point where the Bosporus Strait now enters into the Black Sea. Ryan states: "ten cubic miles of water poured through the Bosporus each day, two hundred times what flows over Niagra Falls." They estimated that the Black Sea rose about six inches a day, taking approximately two years for the Black Sea to reach its current level while the entire sea

---

[163] Earthguide.ucsd.edu/climate change

[164] Gen 7: 11 says "All the fountains of the great abyss burst forth" implying waters came from below the ground as well as from the sky.

[165] William B.R Ryan, Walter B. Pitman, *Noah's flood, The New Scientific Discoveries about the Event that Changed History* (New York, Simon & Shuster, Inc. 1998). Hereafter Ryan/Pitman

[166] Wilson, Chapter 4

level lowered one foot worldwide. About a year after Ryan and Pittman published their theory, Dr. Robert Ballard, famous for photographing the *Titanic*, journeyed to the Black Sea where he photographed and retreaved remains of what was once a wood frame building and stone tools[167] along what appeared to be an ancient shoreline at the level of 300 feet. His photos clearly showed a well-civilized society living there at the time of the flood. Ballard found fresh water mollusks along the sunken beach which were carbon dated to 7000 BC.

What about Noah building the Ark? Ian Wilson, in his book *Before the Flood*, states that the *Black Sea Lake People* would have had almost a year to build a boat to save an extended family and their animals using a reed boat that was in use by the Catal Huyuk civilization living in the area at the time of the flood. With the information we now have from Dr. Finkel's book *The Ark before Noah*, it is quite possible the reed boat surmised by Wilson could have been a round Coracle which according to Finkel was common to ancient and current river dwellers.[168] Such a mammoth endeavor would surely have been a legend to the people of this time and endured in the epics that eventually were written in other parts of Mesopotamia. The description of the Ark is not the same as we see in Genesis, but is interesting that in both cases God/gods directed the construction of the vessel.

What is important to our study of Ancient Sumer is that Ryan and Pittman estimate that as a result of the event the *diaspora* of the Black Sea Lake People may have been into southern Mesopotamia and northern India about 5500 B.C. This is when we first find the Ubaidians civilization in Sumer and the Harappa civilization in the Indus Valley in northern India.[169] This is interesting to us because both civilizations practiced the

---

[167] The same wood frame construction and stone tools were found in the ancient Catal Huyuk civilization. Catal Huyuk was an extensive Neolithic city-state in southern Anatolia from approximately 7500 BC to 5700 BC. (Langer, William L., ed. (1972). *An Encyclopedia of World History* (5th Ed.). Boston, MA: Houghton Mifflin Company.)

[168] See page 69 for a description of the *Coracle reed boat in Finkel's tablet.*

[169] Ibid, Wilson, Chapter five and six.

same polytheism that we find in Ur III at the time of Abraham and in northern India when Hinduism first made its way into written history. This same Hinduism remains the primary religion of India today. Therefore, by observing the spirituality of Hinduism, we may be able to ascertain what the polytheism of Abraham's time would be today. As we have seen, ancient Sumer was highly advanced for this time in history, much more than the nomadic Semites who will eventually replace them in southern Mesopotamia. It seems quite possible that the Ubaidians (who became the Sumerians) were the displaced people from this advanced civilization near the Black Sea.

The Tower of Babel

Genesis tells us that the Semites migrated from the east to Shinar, and after the flood the whole world spoke the same language. After settling in Mesopotamia, the people decided to make their city great in eyes of the world; thus, they began to build a *city with a tower from fire hardened brick held together with mortar and bitumen with its top to the sky*[170] The purpose, it seems, was to make themselves look better than anyone else around them, which in the eyes of God is the sin of pride. Josephus, quoting the Jewish apocryphal book of Jubilees,[171] seemed to blame Nimrod for the building of the tower as we see here:

> "Now the multitude were very ready to follow the determination of Nimrod and to esteem it a piece of cowardice to submit to God; and they built a tower, neither sparing any pains, nor being in any degree negligent about the work: and, by reason of the multitude of hands employed in it, it grew very high, sooner than anyone could expect"[172]

---

[170] Gen 11:1, 4 (NABRE notes suggest that the Tower of Babel was inspired by the Ziggurats of ancient Babylon)

[171] Jub 10:20-21

[172] Josephus, Antiquities 1.4.3

While this action by man angered God, He did not want to destroy the world by flood again. Genesis tells us that He punished man another way by separating them by different languages as seen below:

> *The whole world spoke the same language and the same words.--- Let us then go down and there confuse their language, so that one will not understand the speech of another.*[173]

This separation of language story within the Tower of Babel episode did not seem to have a counterpart in Mesopotamian lore. In 1968, Samuel Kramer in the Journal of American Oriental Society translated the Sumerian epic *Enmerkar and the Lord of Aratta*. Below is a portion of the translation:

> "In those days, harmony-tongued Sumer, the great land of the decrees of prince ship, the whole universe, the people in unison, to Enlil in one tongue [spoke]. [Then] Enki, the lord of abundance [whose] commands are trustworthy, The lord of wisdom, who understands the land, The leader of the gods, endowed with wisdom, the lord of Eridu changed the speech in their mouths, [brought] contention into it, Into the speech of man that (until then) had been one." [174]

It is interesting to note that it took Kramer until 1968 to discover this section of the epic. This makes me wonder if we have just started to discover the depths of knowledge these magnificent works of literature will bring to the study of Scripture. With Kramer's persistence as a scientist, we have a clue as to where the separation of language story in Genesis originated.

---

[173] Gen 11:7

[174] Kramer/History, The clay tablets containing these epics frequently had words and sometimes whole sections missing. The translators usually designate a word they have added in parenthesis as we see in this translation by Kramer. Translators use ...... to indicate missing sentences or sections.

The Book of Job

Many of the tablets found in ancient Mesopotamia that were part of our study were recovered and sold at different times ending up in separate museums or in private collections. Only someone very familiar with cuneiform and Sumerian epics could discover separate tablets as part of one story. One example was when Kramer identified four tablets in the University Of Pennsylvania Museum (where he worked) and two other tablets half way around the world in the Museum of the Ancient Orient in Istanbul as being part of the same 135 line story. When he finished his translation of the combined documents, he discovered the ancient poem was possibly the first essay on human suffering and man's call to God for deliverance. It was a lamentation quite similar to that in the Book of Job.[175] Kramer states:

> "The main thesis of our poet is that in cases of suffering and adversity, no matter how seemingly unjustified, the victim has but one valid and effective recourse, and that is to glorify his god continually, and keep wailing and lamenting before him until he turns a favorable ear to his prayers."[176]

Like the Book of Job, the poem is in four parts. The first introduces the *just man* who has much happiness and possessions, who constantly praises his god. Then the man suffers sickness and misfortunes and petitions his god for deliverance:

> "My god, you who are my father who begot me, lift up my face. ... How long will you neglect me, leave me unprotected?"

The man also suffers mistreatment from his friends and still praises his god. His friends tell him he is suffering because he is a sinner:

---

[175] Pritchard, VII, *Lamentations*. The Sumerians authored *Lamentations* over the destruction of Sumer and Ur. They also authored *Wisdom* literature, *Oracles* and *Prophesies*.

[176] Kramer/History pg. 112

> "They say ... Valiant sages ... A word righteous and
> straightforward: Never has a   sinless child been born
> to its mother."[177]

Finally his god delivers him from his distress and he praises his God for his goodness:

> "The man ... his god harkened to his bitter tears and
> weeping, the young man ... his lamentations and wailing
> soothed the heart of his god. The righteous words, the
> pure words uttered by him, his god accepted. ... The
> encompassing sickness-demon which had spread wide its'
> wings, he swept away. ... He turned the man's suffering
> to joy."[178]

The very interesting part of this story is that the man is pleading with his own *personal* god who acted as the man's personal representative and intercessor with the assembly of gods much as we do today when we petition saints to pray to God for us. It also would seem to be the first written concept of "guardian angels".

Mythology in Genesis

The ancient creation, paradise and flood stories give credibility to the historicity of Genesis more than refute it. Did Abraham bring these mythological stories with him to Canaan? Maybe Genesis itself will give us the answer. There is a very unusual and seemingly out of context story within Genesis—the ***Origin of the Nephilim*** which reads:

> ***When human beings began to grow numerous on***
> ***the earth and daughters were born to them, the sons***
> ***of God saw how beautiful the daughters of human***
> ***beings were, and so they took for their wives whomever***

---

[177] This could be the first written reference to the Catholic dogma of *Original Sin* (CCC 388).

[178] Kramer/History pp. 112-113

> *they pleased. Then the LORD said: My spirit shall*
> *not remain in human beings forever, because they*
> *are only flesh. Their days shall comprise one hundred*
> *and twenty years. The Nephilim appeared on earth in*
> *those days, as well as later, after the sons of God had*
> *intercourse with the daughters of human beings, who*
> *bore them sons. They were the heroes of old, the men*
> *of renown.*[179]

There have been a myriad of explanations of these four lines in Genesis from Jewish and Christian apologists for centuries who until a few hundred years ago assumed a more literal Scripture. Not one of these opinions for this bizarre story gives a reasonable explanation in my opinion. It is informative to read the explanation in the notes of Chapter 6 in the New American Bible Revised Edition which accepts the Historical-Critical method of Biblical studies:

> "The text, apparently alluding to an old legend, shares
> a common ancient view that the heavenly world was
> populated by a multitude of beings, some of whom were
> wicked and rebellious."[180]

How did this very unusual *old legend* end up in Genesis? The explanation continues:

> "It is incorporated here, not only in order to account
> for the prehistoric giants, whom the Israelites called the
> Nephilim, but also to introduce the story of the flood
> with a moral orientation—the constantly increasing
> wickedness of humanity."

This might explain why it was included by the authors and redactor who gave us our current book of Genesis. More important to our study, it gives credence to the existence of detailed ancient legends that may well

---

[179] Gen 6:1-4
[180] New American Bible Revised Edition, 2011

have been brought by Abraham to be carried on through the ages to his descendants. I am not trying to be critical of the authors of the NABRE. I just want to point out that this anomaly in Genesis indicates the Hebrews were aware of the ancient Mesopotamian epics when Moses relayed their history to his people, and this story was just one of the bunch. Somehow, a scribe along the way or the redactor of the Hebrew Scriptures left this story in the book of Genesis, not realizing how uncharacteristic it was to the rest of the Genesis story. And this could only happen if that person was familiar with the Mesopotamian lore. To me, this is the only logical explanation for these scandalous four lines being right in the middle of one of the most sacred books of Holy Scripture.

As we shall see later, the Hebrew people learned to write with an alphabet possibly even before their time in Egypt. There are stories from ancient Mesopotamia, Canaan and even Egypt that may have influenced the Hebrew Scriptures that are not relayed here. I have emphasized the stories from ancient Mesopotamia as this is where Abraham lived and was educated. When God gave Abraham the instruction to leave Ur III and go to the land of Canaan, I believe that he brought these storied with him, making sure that his descendants knew them as well. As we have seen, even Joshua knew that generations prior to Abraham were polytheists. It is quite possible that Abraham is the one that brought this information to him through Hebrew descendants. If so, Abraham was an amazing historian as well as God's prophet.

CHAPTER SIX

LIFE AFTER DEATH

Amen, I say to you, today you will be with me in Paradise. [181]

From the time that human beings had a soul[182] and free will, we intuitively knew that somehow we were superior to the animals around us. We knew right from wrong, animals did not. We also instinctively understood that there was something superior to man that created what we saw around us. Since that time, man has been trying to reason just how this all happened. During the journey he established a set of beliefs to explain all that he saw around him. We call that endeavor religion, and man has been practicing it in one form or another since coming together as a society.

Humanity has progressed technologically far beyond the primitive culture of the Mesopotamians, while our struggle to understand ourselves has had

---

[181] Lk 23:43, Jesus to the repentant thief.

[182] "Soul refers to the innermost aspect of man, that which is of greatest value in him, that by which he is most especially in God's image: *soul* signifies the spiritual principle in man". CCC 364

a similar progression.[183] The ancient Mesopotamians were created with a soul and in the *image of God* just as we are today.[184] As God had not yet disclosed His Plan of Salvation, our anthropomorphic brothers depict man as created by the gods to serve their physical needs. It would seem that the polytheists of the Near East projected what we would call the soul into the gods they created – still not understanding that the spirit within them was created in God's image. The gods were the unanswered question of life that comes with a soul. Much as the artist of today projects his/her soul onto a canvas, poem or song, the ancients projected that same energy into their gods, and that is why they were so real to them. There was a morality within man that established what was right and wrong, and the ancient polytheists projected this innate understanding to their gods giving them human vise and virtues.

The ancient Mesopotamians called the divine spirit that dwelled within each human *the breath of life*. This occurs when the father god Enki puts a spirit within his creation as we read below:

> "Enki opened his mouth and addressed the great gods: I will make a purifying bath. Let one god be slaughtered so that all the gods may be cleansed in a dipping. From his flesh and blood, let Nintu (Enki's assistant) mix clay, that god and man may be thoroughly mixed in the clay, *let there be a spirit from the god's flesh* so that we may hear the drum for the rest of time. Let it proclaim living man as its sign, so that this is not forgotten *let there be a spirit.* "[185]

---

[183] The CCC says this best: "With the progress of Revelation, the reality of sin is also illuminated. Although to some extent the People of God in the Old Testament had tried to understand the pathos of the human condition in the light of history of the fall narrated in Genesis, they could not grasp this story's ultimate meaning, which is revealed only in the light of the death and Resurrection of Jesus Christ." CCC 388

[184] *Imago Dei* (in the image of God) The Church teaches that every soul is created immediately by God – it is not produced by the parents – and also that it is immortal. CCC 366

[185] Arnold/Beyer, *Epic of Atra-khasis*, pg.24

One god is slaughtered, and his flesh and blood are mixed with clay. Then the spirit of the god's flesh becomes the spirit within man. This is clearly the concept of man receiving some sort of spirit from the gods, something we would call a soul. It is interesting that in Chapter 2 of Genesis we find something similar:

> *Then the Lord God formed the man out of the dust of the ground and blew into his nostrils the breath of life, and the man became a human being.*[186]

Theologians who accept the scientific *Theory of Evolution* consider this *breath of life* the instance when God gave developing man a soul. *When* is the question? Before we leave this passage in the creation myth, we cannot overlook the line that says, "let one god be slaughtered so that all the other gods may be cleansed." This same theme is repeated in a later Akkadian creation epic during Abraham's time when Marduk creates man also by slaughtering one god to cleanse the others (probably copied from the earlier Sumerian version). How can we not recall the Crucifixion of one man three thousand years later, which fulfills this prophecy cleansing all of mankind of original sin?

We observe ancient Sumerian's concern for life after death in the *Epic of Gilgamesh* where Gilgamesh begins his epic journey searching for Utnapishtim, who with his wife was the only humans to have found immortality. Eventually Gilgamesh is told by Siduri, the divine wine-maker and brewer, to make the most out of his life for … "the life which thou sleekest thou wilt not find." As there was no hope for immortality, then death meant a descent into nothingness for the spirit and a slow return to dust for the body in the Netherworld. Lest we look down on the ancient Mesopotamians for their despairing theology, all we have to do is look at the many Godless in today's society, who shares the same fate. And they too have created gods in their own image – gods of money, power and fame.

---

[186] Gen 2:7

The Netherworld

To have a *spirit within* is one thing, having an *afterlife* is another. The ancient Mesopotamians did not tell of an afterlife for man although they did have tales of a place for the dead that were quite frightening. This place was called the *Nether World* or *Netherworld*. In Sumerian and Akkadian mythology, Irkalla is the *Netherworld* from which there is no return. It is also called Arali, Kigal, Gizal, and the lower world. The Mesopotamians believed that every man and woman that died, regardless of his or her good or evil on earth, entered this place where the body decomposed into dust. They do not tell us the fate of the *spirit within*, and as there was no anticipation of an afterlife, the time in the Netherworld would be filled with despair. The people, and even their gods, dreaded the Netherworld as only evil gods and demons of the underworld lived in Irkalla.

The Netherworld is ruled by the goddess Ereshkigal and her consort, the death god Nergal. The Sumerian myth, ***Inanna's Descent into the Nether World,*** and the Akkadian later version ***Ishtar's Descent to the Nether World,*** are similar.[187] The story begins when Inanna the queen of heaven (called the great above) wants to visit the Netherworld (called the great below) where her older estranged twin sister ***Ereshkigal*** is its queen. She adorns herself with divine ordinances and queenly robes, jewels and makeup, and sets out for the Netherworld. She is fearful that if she visits there, Ereshkigal will put her to death with all the other inhabitants of this world. She instructs her messenger ***Ninshubur*** to watch for her; and if she does not return after three days and nights, Ninshubur is to go to Enlil, the god of Nippur, to rescue her. If Enlil refuses to come, he is to go to Nanna the moon god of Ur. If he refuses, Ninshubur is to go to the city of Eridu to find Enki, the god of wisdom, who knows the *food of life* and the *water of life*. Inanna descends into Irkalla and has to pass through *the seven gates of the Netherworld* (Dante's Inferno comes to mind) removing some of her jewelry and clothes at each gate until she is completely naked when she comes before Ereshkigal and the ***Anunnaki, the seven dreaded judges of the netherworld*** (and possibly the source of the seven-headed dragon), who give her their *eye of death*. She is then turned into a corpse and hung from a stake. After three days and no Inanna, Ninshubur approaches the

---

[187] The Akkadian version is contemporary to Abraham and would have been the version he was familiar.

three city deities, and the only one who agrees to help is Enki, the god of wisdom. Enki instructs some of his messengers to go to the Netherworld to sprinkle the *food of life* and *water of life* sixty times on Inanna. Inanna is revived and ascends from the Netherworld:

> "When Inanna ascends from the nether world, *Verily the dead hasten ahead of her.*"[188]

The good goddess Inanna seem to remove the bad elements and make the Netherworld a better place for the dead as the story continues:

> "The Anunnaki fled, now the dwellers of the nether world will descend peacefully to the nether world.*"[189]

The *Anunnaki*" appear throughout ancient epics as an assembly of beings with judicial powers who *administer destinies*. They are frequently asked, as a group, to assist the gods in both good deeds and bad, reminding us of good and bad angels. We have seen the Anunnaki in the Netherworld identified as *fallen gods*. We also find them expelled from heaven on a small unimportant Babylonian statue to a King Kuriglazu. It says:

> "Because their king had punished the Anunnaki (because) he had put them out of the … Of all the lands, out of heaven …*"[190]

The Judeo/Christian concept of Satan and his minions as fallen angels being thrown out of heaven after a battle with God's faithful angels is

---

[188] Pritchard, *Inanna's Descent to the Nether World*, pg. 56. Pritchard uses italics to fill in missing words in his translation "Verily the dead *hastened ahead of her*". His notes do not indicate where he assumed this addition. Kramer in his translation does not add these words and makes it clear that Inanna is only allowed to leave the Netherworld if she brings back someone to replace her. She will arrange to bring back her estranged husband god Dumuzi. This is a major difference as Pritchard's translation is a type of Jesus's descent into Hell which does not seem to be the case here.

[189] Pritchard, Ibid.

[190] Pritchard, *The Duties and Powers of the gods*: Inscription on the Statue of King Kurigalzu, pg. 58

quite similar to ancient myth characters such as the Anunnaki. There are additional allegories and similes in many of these ancient stories that make us wonder how much of our concepts of heaven and hell came from the ancient writings of Sumer and Akkad. Were some stories prophesies of things to come? Clearly the Mesopotamians understood the concept of good and evil as their gods all had virtues and vices. As we do today, they thought of heaven being above and the place of the dead below even if heaven was only for the gods and the Netherworld was for mankind. It is likely that Abraham brought this story of the Netherworld to his descendants. We see this in the Jewish concept of *Sheol,* which was as a grave, pit or abode of the dead[191] for both the righteous and the wicked as seen in Isaiah:

> *Once I said, "In the noontime of life I must depart! To the gates of the Sheol I shall be consigned for the rest of my years"*[192]

Josephus in his *Discourse to the Greeks Concerning Hades* gives a descriptive picture of Hades from the perspective of an educated Pharisee Jew in 100 AD. In part he states:

> "Now as to Hades, wherein the souls of the righteous and unrighteous are detained, it is necessary to speak of it. Hades is a place in the world not regularly finished; a subterraneous region, wherein the light of this world does not shine; --- This region is allotted as a place of custody for souls, in which angels are appointed as guardians to

---

[191] The Jewish Encyclopedia even today gives a similar definition: Hebrew word of uncertain etymology (see Sheol, Critical View), synonym of *bor* (pit), *abaddon* and *shaḥat* (pit or destruction), and perhaps also of *tehom* (abyss). It connotes the place where those that had died were believed to be congregated. (http://www. jewishencyclopedia.com/articles/13563-sheol)

[192] Is 38:10, Note gates of the Sheol which is reminiscent of *Inanna's Descent into the Netherworld.*

them, who distribute to them temporary punishments, agreeable to everyone's behavior and manners."[193]

"For there is one descent into this region, at whose gate we believe there stands an archangel with a host; which gate those that pass through do not pass the same way; but the just are guided to *the right hand* and are led with hymns, sung by the angels appointed over the place, into the region of light into which the just have dwelt from the beginning of the world -----. But, as to the unjust, they are dragged by force to the *left hand* by the angels allotted for punishment. The just guided by the *right hand* are taken to a place called *The Bosom of Abraham.*

The author of Ecclesiastes, which is a lamentation of the vanity of all things unless man gives due thanks to the Creator, tells us of the finality of death for man in the eyes of the Jews at the time of the kingdom when he said:

For the living know they are to die, but the dead no longer know anything. There is no further recompense for them, because all memory of them is lost."[194] The death of humans was no better than animals: "*For the lot of mortals and the lot of beast is the same lot: The one dies as well as the other. Both have the same life breath. Human beings have no advantage over the beasts, but all is vanity.*[195]

There is also the interesting *Witch of Endor* story that occurred a few years before Solomon. We see King Saul's request of the witch of Endor to "bring up" the dead prophet Samuel, which implies that the dead are somewhere – probably in Sheol, the Netherworld.[196] Nevertheless, there is very little in

---

[193] Josephus, (William Winston), An Extract out of Josephus's Discourse to the Greeks Concerning Hades, pg. 974
[194] Eccl 9:5
[195] Eccl 3:19-20
[196] I Sm 28:3-20

early Hebrew Scriptures that connect Sheol with an afterlife. The Jewish theology of an afterlife is called *Olam Ha-Ba* (the coming world), and even today this theology is more akin to their ancient Mesopotamian and Canaanite brethren than it is to Christianity or Islam.

Most Jewish apologists use this logic as to why there is little direct discussion of the afterlife in the Torah. From what I have been able to ascertain from reading the ancient texts, at the time of Abraham there was little, if any, theology of an afterlife for the soul or the resurrection of the body – these theologies first appearing in Judaism after the *Babylon Exile and* even here in a form we would not recognize as Christian concepts of afterlife or belief in a soul.

Only after the second Temple period did the Jews consider Sheol to have separate confines for the good and the evil eventually becoming a place of purification and punishment for one's actions on earth.[197] It was during this same time that the Jews first developed the theology of the resurrection of the body. Much of this new theology was the result of Hellenistic influence from philosophers such as Philo of Alexandria[198] who more than any other intellectual of his day combined Greek philosophical traditions with Biblical Judaism to bring into Judaism the concept of the immortal soul and the resurrection of the body. The resurrection is so ingrained in our Christian conscience; we find it hard to understand how the Sadducees[199] of Jesus' time did not believe in the resurrection of the body.[200] This is probably because as strict believers in the Torah they

---

[197] While the Old Testament writings describe Sheol as the permanent place of the dead, in the Second Temple period (roughly 500 BCE-70 CE) a more diverse set of ideas developed: in some texts, Sheol is the home of both the righteous and the wicked, separated into respective compartments; in others, it was a place of punishment, meant for the wicked dead alone. (Longenecker, Richard N. (2003). *Cosmology.* In Gowan, Donald E. *The Westminster theological wordbook of the Bible.* (Westminster, John Knox Press.)

[198] Philo Judaeus (20 BC-50 AD)

[199] A prominent group of Jews in Palestine from 2nd century BCE through 1st century CE; they were probably a smaller but *elite* group, but even more influential than the Pharisees; they followed the laws of the Hebrew Bible (the Torah), but rejected newer traditions. (Wikipedia)

[200] Mt 22:23

did not accept a theology of life after death and resurrection that came to Judaism after the Babylonian Captivity. Even to the Pharisees of Jesus' time, the Netherworld was a holding place until the final resurrection. That is why the Jews to this day try to keep the remains of their dead together in one ossuary so that their whole body will be reunited with their souls in Sheol at the resurrection. It is also the reason that the Resurrection of Jesus is the paramount dogma of Christianity.

Alan Segal in his classic study "Life after Death"[201] in relating the writings of *The Early Rabbis* makes it clear that there is not a clear Jewish theology on the immortal soul or the world to come. In the Talmudic writings and Midrash (Biblical writings or homilies) he does not find the rabbis directly confronting the issue of what awaits the body and soul after death -- most of the discussion being what will happen to individuals and Israel at the resurrection or end-times. One would think that certainly by the time of the great Jewish Rabbi Maimonides in the 12th Century Jewish thought would have developed a concept of life after death similar to the one familiar to Christians. It appears to be just the opposite. According to a current Jewish learning website:

> "Maimonides developed a complicated Aristotelian model
> of the soul. He described a number of faculties of the soul,
> all of which are related to the relationship of a person to
> his or her material environment, perceptions, memories,
> creativity, and desires. Most of these faculties of soul exist
> only in a living human body; with the death of the body,
> they too die. For Maimonides, the only eternal aspects of
> soul are the logical and spiritual speculations and learning
> of a person produced over his or her lifetime."[202]

And as surprising as it may be to Christians who see our Jewish brother as the cradle of our faith, it seems little has changed in Jewish thought on afterlife over the last thousand years since Maimonides opined on this subject. But, let us wander back two thousand years to that day when all

---

[201] Alan F. Segal, *Life After Death, A History of the Afterlife In Western Religions* (New York, Doubleday, 2004), pg. 603-604

[202] Ancient Israelite concepts of soul/ My Jewish Learning. com/bodyandsoul

of salvation history will change and every Jew and Gentile will have a new lease on afterlife.

The Kingdom of God

As all the Apostles were Jews, they would have been well versed in Hebrew Scripture, which clearly describes the Netherworld in a similar manner as the Sumerians and Akkadians before them. *The Apostles Creed* states that Jesus enters Hades for three days after His death on the cross. Christians believe He then brought forth the righteous from Hades into the ***Kingdom of Heaven***. This event is wedged between the Crucifixion and Resurrection and gets little attention in Christian teachings today. In fact, the *descent into hades* (hell) is not repeated in the *Nicene Creed,* which is dogma to both Roman and Eastern Orthodox Catholics.[203] For this reason, I believe Christians sometimes overlook Jesus descended into Hell, which really was one of the greatest events in Salvation History, as it opened up the *Kingdom of Heaven* to all of the just from the beginning of time. I have come to know Abraham so well, as a result of this study, that I can picture Abraham escorted by his descendant, Jesus of Nazareth, from the Netherworld into Heaven where he sits this day as one of God's greatest prophets. We look at Jesus descending into Hell from our Christian perspective and may not realize the immensity of this act in the eyes of people of Jesus' time. To a Jew at the time of Christ, who knew only of the permanence and dread of the Netherworld, this *Good News* (Gospel) would have ignited a hope in their souls of an afterlife. It took them a while, but the disciples of Jesus will finally come to realize the tremendous gift God was giving to mankind: the opening of the *Kingdom of Heaven* to mankind, which until this time was only for the gods.

---

[203] Nonetheless, This tradition remains today as we see in the Catechism of the Catholic Church: *"By the expression 'He descended into Hell', the Apostles' Creed confesses that Jesus did really die and through his death for us conquered death and the devil 'who has the power of death' (Hebrews 2:14) In his human soul united to his divine person, the dead Christ went down to the realm of the dead. He opened Heaven's gates for the just who had gone before him". CCC 636-637*

CHAPTER SEVEN

TERAH LEAVES UR FOR HARAN

Terah took his son Abram, his grandson Lot, son of Haran, and His daughter-in-law Sarai, the wife of his son Abram, and brought them out of Ur of the Chaldeans, to go to the land of Canaan. But when they reached Haran, they settled there. [204]

Scripture does not tell us why Terah moved his family from the city-state of Ur in the south of Mesopotamia to the town of Haran in the north. The geopolitical world in Ur III at his time in history may give some clues. More than likely, the incursions of the Amorites and Elamites into Ur dynasty territories at this time in history would have caused a major immigration away from Ur to the safe havens in familiar parts of Mesopotamia. Perhaps Terah fled north to escape the impending economic collapse of Ur III due to the loss of tax income from the diminishing vassal states. It is logical that Terah, as a highly educated land owner, would have utilized the limited time of peace during the reign of King Shulgi to head north for the only other city that had the moon god, *Sin,* as its chief deity. It is credible that a devotee of *Sin* would move from Ur to Haran at this time in history, as the deities of Mesopotamian cities highly influenced the culture of the people.

With all the fighting in Ur III at this time in history, it is quite possible that Terah's son Haran was killed in battle during one of these wars. Being of

---

[204] Gen 11:31

the land owning class, we can assume that his family was well known in Ur. Josephus, in *Antiquities of the Jews,* states that when Terah's son Haran died in Ur, he was memorialized by the city where " …his monument is shown to this day"[205] Josephus frequently quoted the Hellenistic era historian, Berosus, who wrote of ancient Babylonia. Josephus statement seems to imply that Berosus wrote of this monument although archeologists have not yet unearthed such a find. If Terah was an important citizen of Ur, perhaps his son Haran was among many citizens on a memorial stele for war dead as a result of the Gutian, Amorite or Elamite wars of Ur III. Josephus opined that Terah left Ur on account of the death of his son Haran. He states:

> "Now hating Chaldea on account of his mourning for Haran, they all removed to Haran of Mesopotamia, where Terah died."[206]

Terah, with his extended family, slaves, and property, like most travelers of his day, would have followed either the Euphrates or Tigris Rivers north to his destination. He would have traveled through the Sumerian city-states to the Akkadian city of Agade, the site of the future city of Babylon near modern Bagdad, following the river through the city of Mari. They would cross the Euphrates at Carchemish during low water periods, which is strategically located as one of the few crossing points of the Euphrates River for large caravans. The river is separated by islands at this location, and even today there is a major bridge over the Euphrates River at this site. From there Terah would have turned north along the Bilikh River to the thriving but small city of Haran – a trip of just under six hundred miles. The alternative route would have taken them up the Tigris to Nineveh and then west to Haran. Was a trip of this nature unusual at this time in history? Historians have found a relatively innocuous but interesting lease document from the ancient city of Sippar in southern Mesopotamia, which gives us an answer to this question. From this document it appears that U-Haul did not invent the trailer rental business. This tablet not only reveals the bureaucratic nature of the times, but that there were well-traveled roads all the way to Kittim in Northern Mesopotamia even though the lessee in this transaction was not supposed to go there:

---

[205] Antiquities, 1.6.5
[206] Antiquities, 1.6.5

"A wagon from Mannum-balum-Shamash, son of Shelibia, Khabilkinum, and son of Apparibu on a lease for one year has hired. … Unto the land of Kittim he shall not drive it."[207]

Ancient Haran

Terah's son, Haran, who died in Ur, bears the same name as the city of Haran (sometimes spelled Harran). Some Bible literalists have argued that the town was named after Terah's son as several towns in the area still have Hebrew names. Haran in ancient Akkadian means road or caravan and in Aramean means highway. The city clearly existed centuries before Terah's arrival as it was a main commercial city along the ancient *Silk Route* from Aleppo on the Mediterranean coast to the Far East through Nineveh. It is more probable that Terah named his son after the city of Haran because it was a major pilgrimage destination for the cult of the moon god Sin of Ur III. The several thousand Mari Tablets confirmed that the city Haran, like the ancient Sumerian city of Ur, worshiped the moon god *Sin,* as he was called by both the Akkadians and his daughter, the goddess Inanna. Records also tell us that no other cities along the Euphrates had Sin as their primary deity. Therefore, it is not surprising that Terah's family would choose Haran as a destination and stay there even after Abraham left for Canaan. We know from a stele found in Haran in 1954, which was dated from the time of Daniel's captivity in Babylon, that the god Sin was still worshiped there in the sixth century BC. The following are the first seven lines of the inscription on this stele:

"I (am) the lady Adda-guppi, mother of Nabium-na'id, king of Babylon, Votaress of the gods Sin, Nin-gal, Nusku, and Sadarnunna, my deities who, from my childhood, have sought after their godheads. Whereas in the 16th

---

[207] George A. Barton, *Historical Value of the Patriarchal Narratives,* Proceedings of the American Philosophical Society, 52, April 1, 1913, pg. 197

year of Nabopolassar, king of Babylon, Sin, king of the gods."*208*

While this work assumes (and attempts to prove) that Terah lived in the city- state of Ur during its Third Dynasty, some scholars today opine that the Ur mentioned in Genesis is rather the town of Urfa (ancient name Urrhai) located about 30 miles from Haran in the eastern part of Turkey today. However, as mentioned earlier, Genesis refers to the Hebrew Ur Kasdim, which translated is *Ur of the Chaldees*. Records indicate that the Chaldeans were a people who lived in what is now southern Iraq not earlier than the seventh century BC.[209] This is one of the examples Biblical scholars use as proof that the Hebrew Scriptures were put down in final form after the people of this area were referred to by this name. Josephus also places Terah in the ancient city of Ur. This evidence has led me to conclude Terah lived in the ancient city-state of Ur in its Third Dynasty in 2000 BC.

The Cult of the moon god Sin

It seems that the cult of the moon god Sin was more than just the devotion to a deity. It was a form of scientific study of the stars and the entire solar system wrapped around a devotion to a deity. As we discovered earlier, the moon god is superior to even the sun god in the pantheon. Further, it appears the Sumerian/Akkadians placed their temples to Nanna/ Sin in precise locations by latitudes determined by mathematical and astronomical applications.

---

[208] In August-September of 1956 Dr. D. S Rice made an important discovery at the *Harran* site. Rice was examining the ruins of a medieval mosque when he discovered some Babylonian Stele with inscriptions dating back to the sixth century BC. The stele were turned face down and used as steps at the North, East and West entrances to the Mosque. These are now believed to be part of a set of four inscriptions that probably once hung at the doors to the temple of the Babylonian moon god-Sin. http://www.georgefox.edu/seminary

[209] Chaldean, A member of an ancient Semitic people who controlled S Babylonia from the late 8th to the late 7th century BC, Freedictionary.com

In 1994, archaeologists found an ancient civilization at Gobekli Tepe in southwest Turkey, just 40 km north of ancient Haran. It consisted of several *temples* with large stone-carved monoliths in a circular pattern much like those found at Stonehenge in England – but 7000 years older.[210] Archeologists were stunned to discover that the site was twelve thousand years old. The intricacy of the carvings on the monuments indicated a far more advanced civilization than historians thought existed at this early time in history. James Q. Jacobs, an anthropologist and part time astronomer, was investigating the Gobekli Tepe site on Google Earth. He knew of the moon god Sin's temple at Haran and the Ziggurat at Ur and wondered if there was a relation to the temples at Gobekli Tepe. Google Earth revealed that the latitude at Haran equals Three-fourths atan and the Ziggurat at Ur Three-fifths atan (atan = arc tangent) and that the latitude number at the Ur Ziggurat is an accurate value for pi. The only thing I know for sure about Jacob's statements is that both pi and *atan* are significant in higher mathematics. It is incredible that these mathematical calculations are from a society four thousand years old. He opines that Ur and Haran were therefore:

> "Astronomical observatories and geodetically positioned where the math is easiest. Their local level planes and the rotation axis form triangles with low integer proportions." [211]

Further, the temple at Haran is exactly 40 km from the monolith circles at Gobekli Tepe, which is exactly 1/1000th of the circumference of the earth. This meant that whoever located these three temples may have known the distance to the equator and poles of the earth from mathematical calculations alone, which he found amazing. Jacobs continues:

> "Gobekli Tepe features the oldest known room aligned north-south which is evidence of astronomy in practice."

---

[210] Archaeology Magazine – Nov/Dec 2008

[211] http://jqjacobs.net/blog/gobekli_tepe.html. This site is extremely interesting for more reasons than our study. I highly recommend the reader spend some time reviewing the Gobekli Tepe site to grasp just how advanced this civilization was in 10,000 BC. It puts our study of Abraham 8000 years later in a different light.

The Ur and Haran moon temples evidence a relationship to astronomy and precise knowledge of geodesy – what we call exact sciences. This knowledge would require an extremely high level of math."[212]

From the extant writing of ancient Sumer, it is clear that some people made the study of the stars a science as they left details of astrological star patterns. We will see this later in the study of the destruction of Sodom and Gomorrah in Chapter 8. This advanced astronomy practiced by the devotees of Sin in Ur III shows that the worship of the moon god Sin was more than just picking a god to be your number one. Clearly, the development of astronomy was a major effort within the temple community. Could Abraham have been a scientist as well as a prophet? Josephus comments on this subject in Chapter 7 of *Antiquities*. Here he explains that Abraham claimed that the movement of the sun, moon, and all the heavenly bodies are the result of the actions of the God who created them, not the other way around. He was chastised by the local authorities as we see below:

> "If, said he, (meaning Abraham) these bodies had power of their own, they would certainly take care of their own regular motions; but since they do not preserve such regularity (probably referring to the movement of the planets as seen from earth), they make it plain, that in so far as they cooperate to our advantage, they do it not of their own abilities, but as they are subservient to Him that commands them; to whom alone we ought justly to offer our honor and thanksgiving."[213]

We do not know exactly when God first revealed Himself to Abraham. If God had already spoken to Abraham while still in Ur, it is likely that Abraham would make such an argument against astrology using astronomy, and in doing so, he would have upset the local priesthood. This then became another reason for Terah to move from Ur. Josephus concludes this episode when he states:

---

[212] Ibid
[213] Antiquities, 1.7.1

"...the Chaldeans and the other peoples of Mesopotamia raised a tumult against him, he thought fit to leave that country; and by the assistance of God, he came and lived in the land of Canaan."[214]

The Mari Tablets

In the 1930s, more than 20,000 ancient tablets were found in the Palace at Mari in a city located just south of Haran along the Euphrates River. Most of the tablets were dated from about 1800 BC, which was just shortly after most Biblical scholars place Terah's family in Haran. The Mari Tablets greatly enhanced Assyriolosists' understanding of the geography of the area as they included the names of over 500 locations of towns and cities within upper Mesopotamia.[215] Some of the nearby locations listed near Haran were similar in spelling to some of Terah's clan, such as Serug, Pethor and Nahor. As we remember from Chapter 1, Nahor was Abraham's brother, who stayed in Ur when the clan moved to Haran. Genesis finds him later with Terah's clan in Haran where he evidently stayed after Abraham had left for Canaan. My assumption is that Abraham's brother, Nahor, stayed in Ur to dispose of the family property and later followed the family to Haran.

As we see in Genesis, when Abraham sends his servant back to Haran for a wife for Isaac, there was already a city (probably a village) called Nahor.

The servant then took ten of the master's camels, and bearing all kinds of gifts from his master, he made his way to the city of Nahor in Aram Naharaim.[216]

Terah's father was also named Nahor, and some scholars believe he is the namesake of the town. If Terah's family was of aristocratic stock from Ur, then he would have been welcomed and known within the palace at Mari. Some of the tablets refer not only to the Hebrews ("Hapiru") but also to

---

[214] Ibid

[215] For a detailed history of Mari from a Hebrew Scripture context, I suggest the site: Jewishviruallibrary.org/Mari

[216] Gen 24:10

the Banu Yamina ("Benjaminites"), which means *Sons of the Right* or *Sons of the South*. In the Mari documents these Benjaminites from the north worshiped in the temple of the Akkadian moon god Sin located in the city of Haran. This is one more connection of the moon god Sin/Nanna with the clan of Terah, which could indicate that the move was religiously inspired. While Benjamin was somewhat later in Hebrew history, we know that many of the Hebrews remained in Haran for some time as we see Abraham and Isaac sending back to Haran for wives for their sons. If these records refer to Terah's clan, then he was quite an important figure in his day, and we are looking at the first extra-Biblical record of Abraham's family.

Terah Dies in Haran

Our story of Terah ends after the long trek north from Ur. Terah and his extended family settle in Haran where Terah eventually dies at age 205, as referenced in the Judean version of Genesis. The Samaritan version of Genesis reports that Terah died at the age of 145. Both versions state that Terah died when Abraham was 75 and that he began his trek to Canaan shortly thereafter.[217] Using the ages in the Judean text, Terah would have lived in Haran for sixty years after Abraham left for Canaan. However, according to St. Steven's speech before the High Priest in Acts:

> ***So, he went down from the land of the Chaldeans and settled in Haran. And from there, after his father died, He made him (meaning Abraham) migrate to this land where you now dwell.***[218]

This gives credence to the Samaritan version. The Samaritans claim direct ancestry from Aaron, thereby claiming orthodoxy to the teachings of Moses in their version of the Torah; whereas the Hebrew version, as we have discussed before, could well have been rewritten by the scribes of Judah in the sixth to eighth century BC. We will assume that the Samaritan version of Terah's age is correct and that Abraham left Haran for Canaan sometime after Terah had died. We are unaware of how long

---

[217] See footnote in NAB for Gen 11:32
[218] Acts 7:4

Abraham stayed in Haran after Terah's death, but it would be logical that he stayed until his brother Nahor arrived from Ur with his family.

The Abrahamic Covenant

Let us digress from Abraham's travels to discuss the important theological doctrine of the Abrahamic Covenant. It was given to Abraham in three separate revelations in exchange for Abraham's righteousness (faith) and his acceptance of the revealing God as the God of the Hebrews. The first time God promised Abraham great things was while Abraham was still in Haran when God said:

> *Go forth from the land of your relatives and from your father's house to a land that I will show you. I will make of you a great nation, and I will bless you; I will make your name great, so that you will be a blessing. I will bless those who bless you and curse those who curse you. All the families of the earth shall find blessing in you." – "To your descendants I will give this land.*[219]

Genesis relates three different covenants with Abraham. The first is in Chapter 12 as seen above, then again in Chapter 15 where God says:

> *To your descendants I give this land, from the Wadi of Egypt to the Great River, the Euphrates, the land of the Kenites, the Kenizzites, the Kadmonites, the Hittites, the Perizzites, the Raphaim, the Amorites, the Canaanites, the Girgashites and the Jebusites.* [220]

It is from these two covenants that the Jews obtain the concept of "*the promised land.*" The third covenant had some conditions. God tells Abraham:

---

[219] Gen 12: 1-3, 7
[220] Gen 15:18-21

*This is the covenant between me and you and your
descendants after you that you must keep: every male
among you shall be circumcised.* [221]

The covenants in Chapter 12 and 15 seem to have been written by the
"J" (Yahweh) and "E" (Elohist) sources respectfully. The last covenant in
Chapter 17 seems to be from the "P" (Priestly) source as it outlines the
ritual of circumcision at the eighth day after birth for Abraham and his
family -- both natural and from adoption. Circumcision is the permanent
sign of Abraham's covenant with God to his male descendants and is
known by the Jews as the *brit milah.* [222] Before leaving the issue of Biblical
covenants, one will notice that before these covenants are made, man is
required to sever one or more animals in two parts. In ancient times this
symbolizes what will happen to the party that breaks the covenant. In
Hebrew, the verb to seal a covenant literally means "to cut." Some scholars
believe that the removal of the foreskin in circumcision is a symbol of the
sealing of the covenant with God.

This communication from one God who implies exclusivity must have
been strange to a man whose entire society worshiped a pantheon of pagan
gods. Josephus makes note of this when he says in *Antiquities*:

> "He (Abraham) was a person of great sagacity ------ for
> which reason he began to have higher notions of virtue
> than others had, and he determined to renew and to
> change the opinion all men happened to have concerning
> God, for he was the first that ventured to publish this
> notion, that there was but one God, the Creator of the
> universe; and that, as to other gods, if they contributed
> anything to the happiness of men, that each of them
> afforded it only according to his appointment, and not by
> their own power." [223]

---

[221] Gen 17:10-14 (11-14 give further instructions on circumcision rituals)
[222] *Abrahamic Covenant*, Wikipedia.
[223] Antiquities, 1.7.1, pg. 43

This statement is interesting in more than one way. First, as discussed above, Josephus says Abraham was the first to "publish this notion." Does this imply that Abraham was not only literate but may have written his findings down? Second, Josephus acknowledges the uniqueness of the concept of monotheism to his time. We must remember Josephus is repeating the Jewish tradition at the time he wrote *Antiquities*. But it does reveal the traditions of Abraham by the Jews at the time of Jesus, as *Antiquities* was written shortly after the Temple in Jerusalem was destroyed by the Romans. Now there was to be a God of the Hebrews, a God that Abraham would hear from again when he was being prepared to be the father of a great nation. It is interesting to note that none of the three covenants demand that Abraham accept God as the creator – only that he will be the God of the Hebrews. As we shall see, because of Abraham's pagan culture, his concept of God would be something he was familiar with -- the practice of worshiping one deity among many (monolatry) rather than the monotheistic faith that we know today.

CHAPTER EIGHT

ABRAHAM ENTERS CANAAN

The Lord said to Abram: 'Go forth from the land of your relatives and from your father's house to a land that I will show you.[224]

The Seder Olam has Abraham leaving Haran for Canaan in 1901 BC. Why would someone from Mesopotamia, who most historians would say had a superior culture, want to go to Canaan or Egypt? Maybe it was the weather. Scientists that study climatology have identified a major drought in northern Mesopotamia at the beginning of the Middle Bronze Age (2000-1500 BC), which may have caused a major disruption of Mesopotamian societies causing the Semitic peoples to leave their homes and immigrate into Canaan and Egypt.[225] Abraham's family may have left Haran for the same reason his grandsons would later flee to Egypt from Canaan: because of famine.

A major tenant of Genesis is that God told Abraham to go to the land of Canaan. Historical evidence from ancient Egypt indicates that he may

---

[224] Gen 12:1

[225] Climatologists call this the 4.2 kiloyear event which was one of the most severe climatic events of the Holocene period in terms of impact on cultural upheaval. Starting in 2200 BC, it probably lasted the entire 22nd century BC. It is very likely to have caused the collapse of the Old Kingdom in Egypt as well as the Akkadian Empire in Mesopotamia. Gibbons, Ann (1993). *"How the Akkadian Empire Was Hung Out to Dry"*. Science 261 From Wikipedia

have been going there anyway as part of a major migration of Semites from Mesopotamia into Canaan and Egypt. As we see below from the hieroglyphics found in the tomb of the Twelfth dynasty official Khnumhotep, the Canaanites, called *Asiatics* by the Egyptians (the light skinned people with sheep and goats), had entered into this part of Egypt as early as 1850 BC. The pictograph shows bearded foreigners with what looks like composite bows and what historians have identified as a duckbilled axe delivering *eye-black* to the pharaoh.[226] For the bow and ax to be prominent in the Egyptian scene, they both must have impressed the artist of the painting. Later historians will opine these Mesopotamian visitors introduced these weapons to Egypt. As we shall see below when we study the *Hyksos,* by 1750 BC these same Semites gained political control of the Nile Delta of Egypt. If Abraham entered Canaan from 1900 to 1750 BC, it is possible that he was another in a long line of Semitic immigrants who entered Egypt over a long period of time without the necessity of force. Archeologists have found records that show that one Egyptian official had "95 Asiatics as domestic servants" and another record claimed an official was an "officer in charge of Asiatic troops." Both of these statements are typical of new immigrants into a superior society hiring themselves out as domestics and mercenaries before they eventually

outnumber the local inhabitants.[227] The Amarna Letters confirm an early Mesopotamian migration into Canaan that established their culture throughout Canaan much earlier than scholars thought previously.

---

[226] Image from Gerald Gertoux, Dating *the war of the Hyksos*. The composite bow and duckbilled axe were some of the weapons the Asiatics introduced to the Egyptians, pg. 3 Academia.edu website http://www.academia.edu/2414447/ Dating_the_war_of_the_Hyksos (Hereafter Gertoux/Hyksos)

[227] Ibid, pg. 7

The Hyksos

Who were these Hyksos? The answer may be found in some obscure carvings on a palace wall of an Egyptian queen named Hat-shepsut (1486-1469 BC), who is famous in history as the only Egyptian woman Pharaoh ever listed. In her story she tells of the national embarrassment of the *Hyksos,* who came to control the northeastern part of Egypt as early as 1800 BC.[228] By 1725 BC, they had established a kingdom in the city of Avaris in the northeast corner of the Nile Delta. These invaders, or more likely immigrants into Egypt, were Semites possibly from Canaan. Based on their military hardware they were more likely from northern Mesopotamia. According to the Egyptian historian Manetho[229], an Egyptian historian who wrote in the times of Greek domination of Egypt, "The Fifteenth Dynasty of Asiatic rulers of northern Egypt" (Hyksos) eventually controlled all of northern Egypt. Hat-shepsut's stele tells how she brought this embarrassment of Egypt to an end:

> "I have restored that which had been ruined. I have risen up that which had gone to pieces formerly, since the Asiatics were in the midst of Avaris of the Northland, and vagabonds were in the midst of them, overthrowing that which had been made. They ruled without Re, and he did not act by divine command down to my majesty."[230]

We do not have original copies of Manetho's history of Egypt; therefore, when Josephus Flavius quotes Manetho of this historical event in *Against Apion*, it is the principal record we have of what Manetho wrote on this subject. The Greek name "Hyksos" was coined by Manetho to identify the invaders; however, Manetho mistranslated Hyksos as *Shepherd Kings* which led some to identify them with the Hebrews in Egypt. The Hyksos' kings

---

[228] Hyksos: In Egyptian it means rulers of foreign countries.

[229] Manetho was an Egyptian priest and historian who lived during the Ptolemaic times in the 3rd century BC. He wrote "Aegyptiaca" (History of Egypt), none of which is extant. Although no sources for the dates of his life and death remain, his work is usually associated with the reigns of Ptolemy I Soter (323–283 BC) and Ptolemy II Philadelphus (285–246 BC). From Wikipedia

[230] Pritchard, Egyptian Historical Texts, pg. 231

maintained Canaanite names and worshiped Anath and Ba'al Hadad, the Canaanite gods rather than Re, the Egyptian god. The Hyksos may have had some influence in the use of the term Pharaoh as all kings in Egypt after Hat-shepsut removed the Hyksos they were called Pharaoh.[231] There are some archeological connections to Canaan as well. Gerard Gertoux in his treatise *dating the war of the Hyksos* advises that the Jewish Egyptologist Daphna Ben-Tor, who specialized in the study of Egyptian scarabs[232], says in her book *Orbis Biblicus et Orientalis*:[233]

> "The culture of the Canaanite settlers in the eastern Delta displays a distinct similarity to the material culture found at Middle Bronze Age sites in Palestine and studies of scarabs of the Middle Bronze period from both regions argue for the southern Levant as the place of origin of the Second Intermediate Period foreign rulers in Egypt."

These *Hyksos* came from Mesopotamia, and they came to stay. It is Manetho's story of the Hyksos' invasion through Josephus' book that claims the Asiatics took the northern delta area by force of arms. His theory may be confirmed by the American Egyptologist Herbert E. Winlock,[234] who opines that the Hyksos invaders used modern weapons, unknown to the Egyptians, such as the composite bow, the duckbilled axe (both were on display in the hieroglyphic story of the Asiatics entering Egypt above), a new type of shield, mailed shirts, metal helmets and most importantly,

---

[231] Pharaoh, meaning "Great House", originally referred to the king's palace, but during the reign of Thutmose III (ca. 1479–1425 BC) in the New Kingdom, after the foreign rule of the Hyksos during the Second Intermediate Period, became the form of address for a person who was king. *The Oxford History of the Biblical World*. Michael D. Coogan, ed. Oxford University Press. 1998

[232] This historian showed how scarabs gave clues to cultural habits of the society where they are found.

[233] Daphna Ben-Tor: Scarabs, Chronology, and Interconnections--Egypt and Palestine in the Second Intermediate Period. Orbis Biblicus et Orientalis 27. Fribourg: Academic Press, 2007. 211 pp., pp 1-3

[234] Herbert Eustis Winlock (February 1, 1884 – January 26, 1950) was an American Egyptologist employed with the Metropolitan Museum of Art during his entire Egyptology career. Wikipedia

the horse-driven chariot. The Egyptians must have learned quickly because we find another reference to the siege of Avaris by the Egyptians a hundred and fifty years later when a captain of a Nile vessel told of the Egyptian Pharaoh using a chariot:

> "Thus I used to accompany the Sovereign -- life, prosperity,
> heath! – on foot, following his excursions in his chariot
> when the town of Avaris was besieged--"[235]

The Egyptians also had a drought problem for over a hundred year period in 2200 BC which caused a weakening of the empire. At this time in history the kings in the south of Egypt were also preoccupied with frequent wars from the *Nubians* – a dark-skinned people west of Egypt originally from what is now Sudan. At this time there was also internal strife and times of famine in Egypt. If the Asiatics had even a small presence in the Nile Delta at the time of Abraham, these early Hyksos could have established an enclave of Semites in Canaan (probably at Ashkelon) when Abraham and Sarah entered making it reasonable to explain how they came to know Pharaoh.

Land of Canaan

Canaan includes today's Palestine, Lebanon, part of western Syria and western Jordon. The Amonites, Moabites, Edomites, Israelites and Philistines, (who were culturally different), were all Canaanites. All were Semites except the Philistines, who were thought to be the descendants of the Phoenicians arriving in about 1200 BC. The major cities were Hazor, Megiddo, Shechem, Gezer, Lachish, Jericho and Jerusalem. Canaan is strategically located on the land bridge between the two major civilizations of the ancient Middle East, Assyria/Babylon and Egypt. There were two main north-south roads through Canaan connecting Mesopotamia with Egypt which frequently gave the Canaanites toll tax income.[236] Canaan

---

[235] Pritchard, *The Expulsion of the Hyksos*, pg. 233

[236] The *Via Maris,* which means *way of the sea,* runs along the coast between Egypt and Damascus. It followed the Mediterranean shore most of the way, turning inland towards Hazor across the Jordon into Damascus. The *Kings Highway* ran north and south east of the Jordon River.

offered a buffer state for Mesopotamia and Egypt; therefore, its territory was frequently held hostage by one of the two powers much like Poland has been a place of war between Germany and Russia for the last few centuries. As a result of the major climate change in 2200 BC, the major walled city-states of Canaan gave way to small towns and cities dominated by clans and ethnic groups. We see this later in the Hebrew Scriptures in the books of Joshua and Judges when the Israelites' twelve tribes compete for the mountainous areas of Canaan. Because of its geopolitical location, there was not a unified Canaan until the time of the Assyrian or Egyptian control.

The Ugaritic Civilization

Before its destruction and disappearance in about 1200 BC, there was a city- state on the Mediterranean coast across from the northern tip of Cyprus called Ugarit. This ancient but extinct civilization in Canaan is of great interest to Biblical scholars and our study. In 1928, a Syrian farmer found a flagstone in his field near the town of Lataquia in what is northern Syria today. There was some funny writing on the stone so he took it to the local French authorities, who advised the Bureau of Antiquities in Damascus. What the farmer had found was an old graveyard. This led an archeological team inland where they found the remains of the Middle Bronze Age city of Ugarit, which had disappeared from history but had been mentioned in the writing of the nearby city of Ebla in 1800 BC, and in Egyptian records as far back as Pharaoh Senusret I, who reigned from 1971 to 1926 BC. This was all occurring about the time that Abraham left Haran for Canaan. It is possible that he traveled through Ugarit as it was a port city connecting with the trade routes in Mesopotamia. Archeologists have determined that the city-state of Ugarit abruptly disappeared around 1200 BC. Since this is when the Phoenicians first arrived in the Levant, it is possible that they destroyed Ugarit while they pillaged some Egyptian cities. Recently the *Journal of Archaeology of Tel Aviv* states that sediment studies in the Sea of Galilee show that there was a 150 year drought in Canaan from 1250 to 1100 BC. As we have seen above, long term droughts often caused the collapse of city-states in the ancient Near East [237]

---

[237] *"Pollen Study Points to Drought as Culprit in Bronze Age Mystery"*, New York *Times*, 22 October, 2013, Isabel Kershner.

Found within the destroyed city of Ugarit was a palace, a temple, and most importantly, a library within the city's archives that were written in the Sumerian, Akkadian, Hurritic and Ugarit languages. Most important to our study is that within the temple at Ugarit was found details about the gods of Canaan, El, Baal and Asherah. These gods will compete with the God of Abraham for the souls of the Hebrews for the next thousand years. We will study this subject in detail when we learn about *The gods of Canaan* in Chapter 9.

There were also some interesting letters from about 1400 BC in an altered cuneiform style wherein the ancient Akkadian language had been reduced to thirty characters. As cuneiform characters each represented a sound, these thirty symbols made up what epigraphers believe was the first recorded alphabet. Until Ugarit was discovered, most historians believed that the Phoenicians had developed the first alphabet. According to Dennis Pardee's Studies in *Ancient Oriental Civilization:*

> "While the letters show little or no formal similarity, the standard letter order (preserved in the Latin alphabet as A, B, C, D, etc.) shows strong similarities between the two, suggesting that the Phoenician and Ugaritic systems were not wholly independent inventions."[238]

History first finds the Phoenicians in Egypt in the early 12th century BC. The Egyptians called them the "Sea People" as they were more than likely the Mycenaean Greek culture, who brought the Iron Age and its weapons into Canaan. The Hebrews called them the Philistines. As the main body of Ugaritic literature was composed hundreds of years before the arrival of the Mycenaeans, one would think the Canaanites have a better claim on history's first alphabet even if it was in cuneiform, while the Phoenician alphabet had letters more recognizable to historians.

There is an interesting letter from Ammurapi, the last king of Ugarit, (1215-1180) which may explain what happened to this city that appeared to have such a thriving culture. In the letter the king is pleading for military help from his ally, the Hittite king Alasiya:

---

[238] vol. 60, pp. 181–200, Oriental Institute, 2007

"My father, behold, the enemy's ships came (here); my cities were burned, and they did evil things in my country. Does not my father know that all my troops and chariots are in the Land of Hatti, and all my ships are in the Land of Lukka? ... Thus, the country is abandoned to itself. May my father know it: the seven ships of the enemy that came here inflicted much damage upon us."[239]

Ugarit is in Canaan. What the Syrian farmer found were letters written in Canaan at the time the Israelites had just arrived from Egypt. The letters were a gold mine of information to Biblical scholars, who were able to read firsthand about the cultural and religious interactions of the Canaanites and the Israelites at this critical time in Hebrew history. Ugaritic literature acknowledges Yahweh as the god of the Hebrews calling him *the god of the desert* because that is where the Hebrews came from. One of the most important discoveries of the Ugaritic letters was the closeness of the Hebrew language to that of the Canaanites. Many words were the same and some of the Ugarit letters helped to re-translate many old Hebrew words that had been incorrectly copied by Hebrew scribes. As the Hebrew alphabet is similar to the Ugarit one, it is probable that it evolved from the alphabet of their neighbors.

As we recall from the Book of Samuel when David was alienated from Saul, he hired himself out as a mercenary for the Philistines and performed many raids on Israel's foes.[240] The Ugaritic literature was poetic in nature and David would have been exposed to the Philistine's songs and poems to Dagon, who was known as El in Canaan. Many of the Psalms in the Hebrew Scriptures share the same spirituality as the Ugaritic songs to El. This may be the reason several of the Psalms have references to gods and an assembly of gods.

---

[239] Letter RS 18.147, Jean Nougaryol et al. (1968) Ugartica V: 87-90 no. 24, www.scriba.com/doc/Ugarit. This is an excellent site for Ugaritic History.

[240] 1 Sm 27: 1-12

CHAPTER NINE

THE GODS OF CANAAN

The Israelites did what was evil in the site of the Lord. They served the Baals, and abandoning the LORD, the God of their ancestors, the one who had brought them out of the land of Egypt. They followed other gods, the gods of the peoples around them, and bowed down to them, and provoked the Lord.[241]

*A*braham entered Canaan and was exposed to a new culture. While the Canaanites had a history as far back as 5000 BC (Jericho is considered one of history's first cities)[242], records do not indicate a society as advanced as Akkad at the beginning of the second millennium BC. Language was not a barrier since most of the Near East communicated in the Akkadian language, and the people were also Semites. When it came to religion, Abraham was exposed to a new pantheon of gods. The gods and goddesses of Canaan had roots in Mesopotamian lore – and while the names changed, the chores of the gods were pretty much the same as those in Ur III. Many of the Canaanite deities were similar to the gods of the Amorites, who at

---

[241] Jugs 2:11-12

[242] *The Times of Israel* reported in November of 2013 that highway engineers discovered "an ancient city in the Judean lowlands southwest of Jerusalem that included a six-millennia-old cultic temple and a 10,000-year-old house". http://www.timesofisrael.com/archaeological-dig-uncovers-10000-year-old-building/

this time in history were controlling much of Mesopotamia. There was a moon god **Yarikh,** who was not as domineering to the culture as **Sin** was in Ur III. The main gods of the Canaanite pantheon were **EL,** also known as **El Elyon,** which means god most high; **Athirat,** wife of **El** and mother goddess called the "walker of the sea" who later will be called **Asherah** (a highly controversial figure in Hebrew theology); **Hadad** aka **Ba'al Hadad,** the storm god and bringer of rain, who is called "king of heaven" and the first born of **El. Hadad** was also known as **Ba'al,** which was generic for Lord. Others were **Yam,** the enemy of **Ba'al Hadad**, a sea and river god who is sometimes seen as a seven-headed serpent or Leviathan, who served the same purpose in the chaos of creation as the Sumerian Tiamat; **Kothar-wa-Khasis,** whose name means "skillful and wise" who creates tools and weapons; **Anat,** the sister of **Ba'al Hadad,** who is the goddess of war, the hunt and savagery; **Shapsu,** goddess of the sun and **El's** messenger; and **Mot,** the god of death and the underworld. Mot is the Hebrew word for death, and Yam is the Hebrew word for sea which shows the literary relationship of the two cultures.

The Canaanites had a mythical epic of their gods much like Mesopotamians called the *Ba'al Cycle,* which is a story depicting the changing weather cycles in Canaan. While it is not a cosmology of creation, literary scholars believe it to have been inspired by the *Emuma Elish*[243] -- the Akkadian Creation Epic which was known throughout the Near East. The scribe who transcribed the story identified himself, and more importantly, the king of Ugarit at the time as Niqmaddu, which means it was written between 1350 and 1315 BC. Archeologists found six mostly complete tablets in alphabetic cuneiform in the Ugarit library that tell this interesting story. The story may be original at the time of transmission which would place it several centuries after Abraham; on the other hand, it could well have been an ancient epic recopied as the scribes in Sumer and Akkad did with their classic literature.

In the story, Yam, the god of the sea and chaos, asks El if he can assume the powers of Ba'al Hadad (hereafter Ba'al), the storm god of the land, and assume his title "king of the heavens." El gives his blessing, and Yam attacks Ba'al. This was a miscalculation on Yam's part because Ba'al obtains

---

[243] *Emuma Elish* is the first two words of the epic. Many ancient stories will be titled this way.

two magical weapons from Kothar-wa-Khasis called a *Driver* and a *Chaser,* which he uses to strike Yam on the chest and forehead slaying him (these epics are very graphic in depicting violence and mayhem). Yam was known to have a palace in the sea, so Ba'al decides he wants a palace on land. With the help of his sister Anat he convinces El to have Kothar-wa-Khasis build him a palace, which he does with gold, silver and the *cedars of Lebanon.*[244] Ba'al, with bravado, yells out of his palace window challenging Mot, the god of the underworld. This too was a big mistake as Mot enters the window of the palace and swallows Ba'al taking him to the underworld. The Canaanites believed that when a body dies, the *nps* or soul departs from the body to the land of Mot[245]. The readers of the Ba'al Cycle in Canaan would have understood this to be Ba'al's fate in Mot. With Ba'al not present to bring rain, there is a terrible drought causing much pain in the pantheon. All the gods want Ba'al back so they can have rain. So, El allows Anat, Ba'al's sister, to go to the underworld where she earns her title of goddess of savagery as she … "uses a knife to slice Mot into pieces, which she scatters in the wind." With Mot defeated, Ba'al is allowed to return to earth and bring back the much needed rain.[246]

The Canaanites believed that Ba'al's death just before the dry season and his resurrection just before the rainy season is a cyclical event that occurred each year thus the name of the epic. There is much discussion within the Biblical scholar community as to whether this "rebirth" in the *Ba'al Cycle* is the basis for the "imagery of death and resurrection" in Chapters 5,6,13 and 14 of Hosea, which refer to Israel's exile and restoration."[247] This is just one of many Ugaritic theological concepts that may have been adopted by the Hebrews early in their stay in Canaan.

---

[244] Cedars of Lebanon: These legendary trees were brought by King David to build the Temple because of their lasting and pleasant odor. They are mentioned 83 times in the bible. The cedar tree is still the symbol of Lebanon although they are endangered now and highly protected today in Lebanon.

[245] Alan F. Segal, *Life after Death: a History of the Afterlife in Western Religions* (New York, Doubleday, 2004)

[246] Arnold/Beyer, Ba'al Cycle, pg. 50-62

[247] John Day, *Yahweh and the Gods and Goddesses of Canaan,* (Sheffield Academic Press, Ltd New York, 2002), pg. 117

The Ba'al Cycle may also have been inspired by the 150 year drought in Canaan in 1200 BC that we spoke of in Chapter 8 where climatologists examined sediment of pollen in the Sea of Galilee, giving them information enough to pinpoint the time frame.[248] The recent emphasis on the study of climatology has led to many recent discoveries that these droughts in the ancient world caused catastrophic destruction of whole cultures and led to major migrations into less hostile climates, which could have contributed to Abraham coming to Canaan in the first place.

The god El

When Abraham ventured into Canaan at the beginning of the second millennium, we do not know how far polytheism had evolved into the worship of one supreme god among many (monolatry). Most of the academic studies of the gods of Canaan emphasize the late second millennium, after the Hebrews had arrived back in Canaan from Egypt. Hebrew Scripture gives us a clue, however, that El was the name for God in Abraham's time where in chapter 6 of Exodus we find:

> **Then God spoke to Moses and said to him: I am the Lord. As God the Almighty I appeared to Abraham, Isaac, and Jacob, but by my name, Lord, I did not make myself know to them.**[249]

As seen in the Ba'al Cycle, clearly by the 14th century BC the god El had become a primary god controlling the actions of the other gods in the pantheon. The pantheon of Canaan, found in the Ugaritic texts, is called Elohim, which means the children of El or the children of god. El is referred in Ugaritic literature as "Bull El" or the bull god, "creator of creatures and mankind," and *"creator eternal"* which would indicate that by this time in history, the concept of a creating god, was beginning to enter Canaanite polytheism. There is a single tablet found at Ugarit titled

---

[248] *"Pollen Study Points to Drought as Culprit in Bronze Age Mystery"*, New York Times, 22 October, 2013, Isabel Kershner.

[249] Ex 6: 2-3, Footnotes adds the words "as El Shadday" Abrahama, Isaac and Jacob, which means "El of the Mountain". Most Jews do not consider Abraham a Jew as he had not received the Mosaic law..

"El's Drinking Party"[250] which displays he was quite promiscuous in his early days, which will become an issue when he is compared to Yahweh in many scholarly studies. It is interesting to note that in the Ba'al Cycle, El is sometimes mentioned with *the assembly in council* which would seem to indicate a bi-cameral ruling authority within the pantheon as we see here:

> "Do not fall at El's feet, do not prostrate yourself before
> the assembly in council; still standing speak your speech,
> repeat your message; and address the bull, my father El,
> repeat to the assembly in council."[251]

An *Assembly of gods* would be nothing new to Abraham since the epic stories of Sumer and Akkad frequently referred to gods conspiring together. One superior god within the pantheon established a new dynamic in polytheism, creating a four-tier hierarchy within the assembly. The first place was held by the supreme god and his consort such as Ea in Akkad and El in Canaan. The second place is held by the royal children, the third place is held by gods who serve the royal family, and the fourth place is held by minor deities who assist all the gods such as messenger-gods.[252] This pantheon was anthropomorphic since it was arranged along the same lines as their society. There are signs that the Israelis, who lived among the Canaanites, also placed their God within an assembly of gods. In Psalm 82:1 and 6-7 we see Elohim within the divine council when he tells the other gods they will all die:

> *God (Elohim) rises in the divine council; gives judgment*
> *in the midst of the gods.*
>
> *I declare, 'Gods though you be, offspring of the most*
> *high all of you, yet like any mortal you shall die; like*
> *any prince you shall fall.'*

---

[250] *Stories from Ancient Canaan*, Second Edition, Michael D. Coogan, Mark S. Smith, (Westminster, John Knox Press, Louisville, 2012), pg. 167-172

[251] Arnold/Beyer, Ba'al Cycle, pg.50

[252] Mark S. Smith, *The Origins of Biblical Monotheism* (New York, Oxford Press, 2001), pg. 45-46 Mark S. Smith was the President of the Catholic Biblical Association of America in 2010-2011.

We again find a reference to divine sons of God most high (Elohim) in Deuteronomy where it says:

> *When the Most High allotted each nation its heritage, when he separated out human beings, He set up the boundaries of the peoples, after the number of the divine beings; but the Lord's portion was his people; his allotted share was Jacob.*[253]

Note that the gods are offspring of the most high, and are arranged in level one and two in the Israeli pantheon, similar to the pantheon of El. It is interesting to note that in the translation of this Scriptural quote in the Masoretic text they change the words "divine sons" to "sons of Israel," which we assume is due to the clear reference to polytheism.[254] The early references to a hierarchy of gods in the Hebrew Scripture make me believe that when Abraham entered Canaan (a thousand years prior to the authors of the Psalms and Deuteronomy); a hierarchy of gods was part of his understanding of deity.

El in the Hebrew language is generic for God. Archeologists found temples to Ba'al and Dagon in the ruins of Ugarit, but none to El. This leads some scholars to opine that Dagon, who like El is depicted as the father of Baal, may have been another name of El. While El is called a creator, to date scholars have yet to find evidence within Canaanite literature of a cosmology describing the origin of the universe. The Historian Philo of Byblos (64-141 AD) claims to have received, from Sanchuniathon of Beirut, a mythology story that describes a creating deity named Elion, the father of the gods, who was married to Beruth from which we obtain the name for the city Beirut in Lebanon. While we do not have an extant copy of this epic, most of the Ugaritic literature seems to have a Mesopotamian root; therefore, we can assume there was a cosmology story of some sort.

While the epic stories of Canaan identified El as a supreme god, this deity was still not a transcendent, boundless God above human understanding as he was still created in man's image. El and the other supreme gods of Mesopotamia were usually depicted as old, retired and very wise as we

---

[253] Dt 32:8-9, Smith/Origins pg. 48
[254] Ibid

observed in Sumer when Enki assumed this role and Ea became the father of the gods in Akkad. When Abraham entered Canaan, El had assumed this role. Ba'al seems to become the primary god in later Ugaritic literature, pushing El to the side as a grandfather figure. The gods El and Ba'al were important deities in Canaan not only when Abraham entered in 1900 BC, but also when his descendants returned from Egypt five hundred years later. And, as we shall see, El and Ba'al, who will later assume a greater role in the pantheon, will have a great influence on Abraham and his descendants.

Ba'al Hadad, the Rider of the Clouds

Before we study Ba'al Hadad of the Ba'al Cycle, we need to know more about the term Ba'al. The Catholic Encyclopedia defines Ba'al as "a Semitic word meaning 'lord' in the connotation of ownership of say a house, a field, of cattle, of wealth, even of a wife – which is the reason in the Hebrew language we do not find a woman being called *Ba'alah of her husband*."[255] When we find the Hebrews worshiping or building altars to Ba'al, it could be the Ba'al of Lebanon, who is Cid; or Hadad, who is the god of storms and rain in Canaan, or Dagon, the god of the Philistines. As we see from the book of Judges at the head of this chapter: The children of Israel offended the Lord by serving the Ba'als. In this quote the offending god is plural. So, we do not know the specific gods the Hebrews worshiped at this time.

There is a figurine of Ba'al in the Louvre which was found in the ruins of Ugarit from the 12-14th century. It shows Ba'al with a raised right arm and his left foot forward, which is exactly the way the Egyptian god *Set* is depicted. Further, Ba'al is always shown wearing the crown of Lower Egypt. Ugarit, being on the coast of the Mediterranean Sea, had been invaded by Egypt in its past, and there were many artifacts found in Ugarit that have Egyptian origins which would account for this unusual image of a Canaanite god. It also could mean that Egypt had a great influence on the theology of Canaan.

Ba'al Hadad was the storm god, a god of rain, thunder, fertility, agriculture, and the lord of heaven. We see him called the "Rider of the Clouds" in

---

[255] Catholic Encyclopedia, *Ba'al*, Kevin Knight, 2002

the Ba'al Cycle.[256] The Hurrians, whom Abraham would have known as Gutians, had a storm god named Teshub; and the Hittites, from what is now Turkey, had a storm god named Tarhunt, which shows that the Hittites, like the Egyptians, left their mark on Ugaritic culture. It seems clear that the rain cycle played a major role in the pantheon of gods in Canaan as well as Mesopotamia. A Christian who knows his Bible will recognize a God who "Rides the Clouds." After all, Jesus ascended into heaven on a cloud and will return the same way.[257] There are also the following scriptural passages that refer to a Yahweh who rides the heavens or the clouds:

See the Lord is riding on a swift cloud on his way to Egypt.[258]

Who rides the heights of the ancient heavens[259]

You make the clouds your chariot; traveling on the wings of the wind[260]

And we see in the *Ba'al Cycle*: [261]

"Kothar-wa-Khasis replied: Let me tell you Prince Ba'al, let me repeat, Rider of the Clouds." (pg. 51)

"Astarte shouted Ba'al's name: 'Hail Ba'al the Conqueror! Hail Rider on the Clouds.'" (pg.52)

"What enemy has risen against Ba'al, what foe against the Rider of the Clouds?" (pg. 53)

---

[256] Arnold/Beyer, *Ba'al Cycle*, pg. 53

[257] Acts 1:9-11

[258] Isaiah 19:1

[259] Ps 68:34

[260] PS 104:3

[261] Arnold/Meyers

Further, in Daniel 7 there is a clear prophesy of the Son of God uniting with God the Father as there is anywhere in the Hebrew Scriptures:

> *As the visions during the night continued, I saw coming with the clouds of heaven One like a son of man. When he reached the Ancient of Days and was presented before him, He received dominion, splendor, and kingship; all nations, peoples and tongues will serve him. His dominion is an everlasting dominion that shall not pass away, his kingship, one that shall not be destroyed.* [262]

This passage was obviously well known and important to the Jews as we see when Jesus is before the Sanhedrin and is asked if He is "the Messiah, the Son of God." Jesus answers:

> *"From now on you will see the Son of Man seated at the right hand of the Power and coming on the clouds of heaven." Then the high priest tore his robes and said, "He has blasphemed! What further need have we of witnesses? You have now heard the blasphemy."*

Clearly the Sanhedrin knew Jesus was referring to Daniel 7 because in unison they all said *"He deserves to die."* [263]

Dr. Michael S. Heiser in his excellent article, *What's Ugaritic Got to do with anything?* [264] Analyzes the similarities of the Ugarit Ba'al Cycle with Daniel 7. Here is a paraphrase of his analysis:

1. El, the aged high god, is the obvious leader of the *assembly in council*, while in Daniel 7, *The court was convened, and the books*

---

[262] Dan 7:13-14

[263] Mt 26:64-66

[264] Michael S. Heiser, PhD, *"What's Ugaritic Got to do with anything?* https://www. logos.com/ugaritic. Dr. Heiser's article explains the great help the Ugaritic letters gave to bible scholars in correcting some miscommunications from Hebrew scribes. I highly recommend the reading of his whole article.

were opened and *The Ancient One* (Yahweh) *is seated on the fiery, wheeled throne.* Both the Ugaritic text and Daniel depict God as white haired and aged and both show an assembly in heaven.

2. El bestows "eternal kingship and dominion" *on Ba'al*, "Rider on the Clouds" after Ba'al defeats Yam, while in Daniel 7, **the Ancient One bestows dominion, glory and kingship upon the son of Man, who is coming on the clouds of heaven after the beast was slain and its body was thrown into fire to be burnt up** (which also occurred in the Ba'al Cycle).

3. El is the father of the pantheon at the same time that Ba'al is "king of the gods," implying two thrones. Daniel 7 says: **Thrones were set up** and later the **Ancient one took His throne** (singular). *The Son of Man* is given everlasting dominion over the nations. He and God have dominion much like El and Ba'al in the Ugaritic text. This part of Daniel clearly refers to God the Son as the second person of the Blessed Trinity to Christians, but is an anathema to Jews and Muslims who have a difficult time explaining the use of the plural thrones.

Yahweh, God of the Hebrews

Some will have difficulty accepting that Yahweh, the God of the Hebrews, had any relationship to the pagan gods El or Ba'al. There are dozens of books by highly qualified Biblical scholars arguing this point; and by no means, do any of their opinions agree. Some say Yahweh and El are the same God, and other say they are not. Some say that Yahweh, like El, had a consort (the Asherah); and others vehemently deny this claim. There is much discussion of the perspective of the authors of the *four sources* having a lot to do with these divergent theories. In some, El is the God of the Hebrews in early Genesis while Yahweh is the God of the Hebrews by other sources. Much of my research on this subject is from two books by Mark S. Smith, *The Early History of God*[265] and *The Origins of Biblical Monotheism*[266], and John Day's *Yahweh and the Gods and Goddesses of*

---

[265] Mark S. Smith, *The Early History of God*, (Grand Rapids, Michigan), 2nd Edition by W.B. Eerdmans Publishing Co., 2002 (Hereafter, Smith/History)

[266] Smith/Origins

Canaan."[267] These books footnote the dozens of published books on this subject by highly respected Biblical scholars from the beginning of the Historical Critical period in the 18th century to today.

The discovery of the Ugaritic literature has dramatically changed the way Biblical scholars look at this subject. Since that time, most scholars believe in the integration of the Canaanite gods into the Hebrews' concept of deity. The arguments seem to be *when* the integration occurred not *if* it occurred. Mark Smith identifies two major factors that influenced the Hebrew understanding of El and Yahweh as ***Convergence*** and ***Differentiation***.[268] He states:

> "**Convergence** involved the coalescence of various deities and/or some of their features into the figure of Yahweh. This development began in the period of the Judges and continued during the first half of the monarchy. --- Features belonging to deities such as El, Asherah, and Ba'al were absorbed into the Yahwistic religion of Israel."

Prior to the discovery of the Ugaritic literature, scholars believed Israel was a separate and foreign society within Canaan. Post-Ugarit scholars are now convinced that the Hebrews were in fact a part of the Canaanite culture and only broke away later under what Smith calls *differentiation.* Smith continues:

> "The second major process involved the ***differentiation*** of Israelite cult from its Canaanite' heritage. Numerous features of early Israelite cult were late rejected as 'Canaanite' and not-Yahwistic. This development apparently began first with the rejection of Ba'al worship in the ninth century BC, continued in the eighth to sixth centuries with the legal and prophetic condemnation of

---

[267] John Day, *Yahweh and the Gods and Goddesses of Canaan*, (Sheffield Academic Press, Ltd New York, 2002 Sheffield Press, 2002 (hereafter Day/Gods)

[268] Ibid pg. 7-9

Ba'al worship, the asherah[269], solar worship and the *high places.*"

If the reader is interested in a deeper understanding of the role of Canaanite deities in early Hebrew theology, I suggest you go directly to the books mentioned. They are highly researched and make a clear picture of the Yahweh within the Hebrew Scriptures with much of His early anthropomorphic nature being from the polytheism around them. This being said, this is a study about Abraham. While some of the convergence of polytheism into the worship of Abraham's God may have occurred in his day, any differentiation from the Canaanites came after the Hebrews returned from captivity in Egypt and Yahweh had become the God of the Hebrews demanding exclusivity of worship.

---

[269] Asherah was El's wife. Many scholars but certainly not all, opine that early Yahweh too had a wife or consort called "the asherah". The idea of God having a wife was an anathema to early biblical scholars. Therefore, there is still considerable debate on this subject.

CHAPTER TEN

ABRAHAM IN CANAAN

Abram was seventy-five years old when he left Haran. Abram took his wife Sarai, his brother's son Lot, all the possessions that they had accumulated and the persons they had acquired in Haran, and they set out for the land of Canaan.[270]

Now that we know a few things about Canaan and the gods of Canaan, we will continue Abraham's journey from Haran into the *Promised Land*. Genesis does not tell us the route Abraham chose to enter Canaan. We can surmise from the trade routes of the time that he forded the Euphrates River at Carchemish, which was on the road from Haran to Aleppo. Once across the Euphrates, he would have proceeded south past Aleppo down to Damascus. According to Josephus, Abraham stopped in Damascus on his way to Canaan and became a person of great importance there. Josephus quotes a contemporary historian, Nicolaus of Damascus:

> "Abram reigned at Damascus, being a foreigner, who came with an army out of the land above Babylon, called the land of the Chaldeans. ---- Now the name of Abram is even still famous in the country of Damascus: and there is shown a village named for him, The Habitat of Abram."[271]

---

[270] Gen 12:4-5
[271] Antiquities, 1.7.2, pg. 74

When the historian Nicolaus says that Abraham came to Damascus with an army out of the land of Babylon, we can make two assumptions: first, he was not just a nomad passing through Damascus but rather the leader of a large group of immigrants; second, that he might have been a trained military leader. There is also the possibility that Nicolaus was referring to the time where Genesis states Abraham came to Damascus with an army of 318 men to slay the leader of the Awan dynasty, who had captured Lot in Sodom in the war of *the four kings against the five.*[272]

If Abraham did pass through Damascus, he would have entered Canaan from the east after crossing the land of Bashan by fording the Jabbok River where it meets the Jordan. He then would have followed the Wadi Farah to Shechem where Abraham built an altar:

> *Abram passed through the land as far as the sacred place at Shechem, by the oak of Moreh. The Canaanites were then in the land. The Lord appeared to Abraham and said: To your descendants I will give this land. So Abraham built an altar there to the Lord who had appeared to him.*[273]

There is a lot to learn from these few lines in Genesis. First, the city of Shechem was an ancient holy city in the hills of Canaan at a crossroad controlling major north-south and east-west roads. It is located at the base of Mount Gerizim and Mount Ebal. This location became very important to the Jews of the Exodus as it was captured from the Canaanites by none other than Joshua:

> *Later, on Mount Ebal, Joshua built to the Lord, the God of Israel, an altar.*[274]

Second, in the eyes of the Jews, God gave what is now the State of Israel to them through these lines in Genesis. In a statement of prophetic irony,

---

[272] Gen 14:9, we will see more of this incident later in this chapter.

[273] Gen 12:6-7

[274] Jos 8:30

God prefaces His promise to Abraham by saying: **the Canaanites were then in the land.** Evidently, this was an issue then as it is even more now.

Genesis tells us Abraham moved from Shechem to the hills east of Bethel just north of Jerusalem where:

> **He built an altar there and invoked the Lord by name.**"[275] This is the same Bethel that **Jacob poured oil on top of it. He named that place Bethel, whereas the former name of the town had been Luz.** [276]

Bethel means the *house or temple of El* (the house of God). As Jacob renamed Luz to Bethel, it is clear he was using the Canaanite word El to describe the God of Abraham. The Hebrews will use the Canaanite word El for God, as we see God referred to as **Elohim** by the E source of the Hebrew Scriptures, who are from the northern kingdom of Israel where Bethel is located. It is much later that Moses will call Abraham's God "Yahweh." We will see the Hebrews using the suffix "el" on many names and places in Hebrew Scriptures. For instance, it is said God gave Jacob the name Israel because Jacob wrestled with the Angel of God, and the Hebrew word for wrestle is the verb **isra,** and **El** is the word for God. Genesis refers to this name change after Jacob's *struggle* with the Angel" where the angel dislocated his hip:

> **Then the man said, "You shall no longer be named Jacob, but Israel, because you have contended with the divine and human beings and have prevailed."**[277]

Whatever the reason, El is the root of the name Israel as El was clearly considered the god of the Canaanites when Abraham arrived, and most likely, the Hebrews used the word El to describe Abraham's God as well. John Day, in his book *Yahweh and the gods and goddesses of Canaan*[278], would agree with this opinion when he states:

---

[275] Gen 12: 8
[276] Gen 28: 18-19
[277] Gen 32:29
[278] Day/Gods, pg. 13

"in that both the E and P sources imply that the patriarchs did not know the name Yahweh and that it was first revealed to Moses (Ex 3:13-15) in contrast to the J source, where the name Yahweh was already known in primeval times according to Gen 4:26".

It appears that Abraham and his clan did not stay long in Bethel as:

He journeyed on by stages to the Negeb. There was a famine in the land; so, Abram went down to Egypt to sojourn there.[279]

It was at this time that Abraham met with the Pharaoh and told him that Sarah was his sister (actually she was his half-sister by Terah's other wife). Abraham uses this excuse a second time in Chapter 20 of Genesis when Abraham told Abimelech, the Philistine King of Gerar, the same story. Abraham must have made peace with Abimelech as Genesis states:

Abraham resided in the land of the Philistines for a long time.[280]

The Philistines[281] were that group of non-Semites that the Egyptians called the "Sea People" who many scholars believe arrived in southern Canaan at the beginning of the Iron Age (circa 1175 BC) probably from the Aegean Sea area. They controlled five cities in southern Canaan with their capital in the ancient port city of Ashkelon. Therefore, in the nineteenth century BC, the Philistines had not yet arrived in Canaan.[282] So, who were these people that Abraham resided with for many years and why were they called

---

[279] Gen 12: 9-10

[280] Gen 21: 34,

[281] The etymology of the word Philistine into English is from Old French *Philistin,* from Classical Latin *Philistinus,* found in the writings of Josephus and Philo, from Hebrew *Plištim,* (e.g. 1 Samuel 17:36; 2 Samuel 1:20; Judges 14:3; Amos 1:8), "people of Plešt" ("Philistia"); cf. Akkadian *Palastu,* Egyptian *Parusata.*

[282] Like the *Chaldeans* of Mesopotamia, they author of Genesis projected his knowledge of the Philistines in this area back to the time of Abraham even though they were not known as Philistines at this time in history.

Philistines? It is implied in the Hebrew Scriptures that the Philistines of David's time were not Semites or even Canaanites and somehow separate from the local population, which would mean that Abraham resided with a non-Canaanite people. We have seen that there was a migration of Semitic people from Mesopotamia into Canaan and Egypt even before Abraham arrived in Canaan. It then seems logical that Abraham "resided for many years" with a non-Canaanite people who most likely were the vanguard of the Hyksos from Mesopotamia. This would answer the question of how Abraham was known by the Pharaoh who coveted Sarah.

There is a third time in Genesis when Isaac also lies to King Abimelech of Gerar (probably the son of the king Abraham met), saying that his wife was his sister for the same reason.[283] This is an example of a *triplet* story in Genesis that we discussed in the introduction concerning *who wrote the Bible*. Bible scholars attribute the first story in chapter 12 of Genesis when Abraham meets Pharaoh and then subsequently with Isaac in chapter 26 of Genesis to the J source (Yahwist – Juda) while Abraham's meeting with Abimelech from the E Source (Elohist- from the Northern Kingdom). The question arises: How was Abraham and his wife Sarah able to travel to Egypt during the famine described in chapter 12 of Genesis to have Sarah taken into Pharaoh's harem?[284] Even if it was fifty years after Abraham entered Canaan, it would put him before Pharaoh in about 1850 BC. If he was known to Pharaoh, possibly the migration of the Hyksos into Egypt had begun as early as Abraham's time.

Abraham the Warrior

Shortly after they entered Canaan, Abraham and his brother's son, Lot, chose to go their separate ways. Abraham gave Lot the first choice; and Lot chose Moab east of the Jordan, the location of the ancient cities of Sodom and Gomorrah. Abraham chose the land of Canaan. Later in Abraham's life in Canaan, the kings of Sodom and Gomorrah[285] rebelled

---

[283] Gen 26:6-11

[284] Gen 12: 10-20

[285] Gen 14:1 the five Canaanite kings of this story are these: *Bera king of Sodom, Birsha king of Gomorrah, Shinab king of Admah, Shemeber king of Zeboiim, and the king of Bela (that is Zoar).*

against the taxation and fealty owed to the king of Elam, who controlled the *Tin Route* from Mesopotamia to Egypt, which ran through Sodom in what is called *The Battle of Siddim*. The Elamite king, Chedorlaomer (aka Chodorlahomor) and three other kings[286] came to the area on a policing action to return the cities to their vassal status. During the sacking of Sodom, Lot was taken captive and taken north towards Babylon along with the forced collection of taxes in the form of booty. Genesis tells us that Abraham established an army of ***318 of his retainers, born in his house,***[287] defeating Chedorlaomer in the city of Dan, which is found today in northern Israel. He then chased the Elamites up to Hobah just outside of Damascus where he killed Chedorlaomer.[288]Here is an example of where secular history and the Hebrew Scriptures combined give us a much clearer picture of this incident. As we discovered earlier, Abraham settled in what is a non-Canaanite community in or near Ashkelon along the sea coast probably in a pre-Hyksos community of Semites from Mesopotamia. When Lot was captured, it seems quite likely that some of Lot's people escaped and came to Ashkelon to tell Abraham of Lot's capture. The Elamite king would have returned back to his homeland north along the Jordon River road to Damascus which would have taken Chedorlaomer into Dan in the wooded foothills of Mount Hermon on his way to Damascus. Abraham and his 318 men would have had a shorter trip up the Via Maris road to Damascus along the sea coast until it joins the Jordon River road at Dan. If Abraham marched all night he could have been able to set a trap for the Elamites at Dan, as stated in Genesis, causing the king to flee north towards Damascus where Abraham slew him just outside of Damasus. Abraham attacked a much larger force of Elamites at night, using what

---

[286] Ibid, The four Mesopotamian kings are these: *Amraphel king of Shinar (Southern Mesopotamia,), Arioch king of Ellasar (northern Mesopotamia, possibly the Gutians), Chedorlaomer king of Elam* (western Persia*), and Tidal king of Goiim (another word for 'nations' – could be Hittites)* (Wikipedia)

[287] Gen 14:14, If Abraham "who resided with the Philistines for many years" lived within a conclave of early Hyksos, he would have had ample military hardware and trained warriors to choose from.

[288] Gen 14 does not say that Abraham killed Chedorlaomer when he defeated him; but we can assume he did so as the abrupt death of the Awan king Kutur-Lagamar (who initiated the action against Sodom and Gomorrah) was 1954 BC -- which fits into the dates in the Seder Olam for the time Abraham was in Canaan and the story of the *five kings against four* in Genesis.

we could call today *special forces*, defeating Chedorlaomer and taking back not only Lot but the booty as well. Traditional Judeo/Christian literature pictures Abraham as a shepherd leading a flock. So how did Abraham find 318 men and leads them into a successful and evidently highly thought out military campaign? This amount of soldiers is the size of a small battalion which would require several specialties such as archers, swordsmen and possibly chariots. How could a shepherd accomplish such a thing unless he had experience? Perhaps the answer lies in the words of the historian Nicolas of Damascus that we saw earlier:

> "Abram reigned at Damascus, being a foreigner, who came with an army out of the land above Babylon, called the land of the Chaldeans[289]

This quote seemed highly unlikely if it referred only to Abraham coming out of Babylon into Canaan; however, it could have been referring to the military action against Chedorlaomer.

Many secular historians, and some Biblical scholars, deny the *four kings against five* battle ever happened, saying that it had nothing to do with Abraham's journey into Canaan. The fact that Abraham brings the spoils from defeating Chedorlaomer to Melchizedek, the king of Salem, who is clearly accepted by the author of Hebrews, [290]would argue against this denial. Doubters of this story also claim that the names of the kings listed in Genesis do not match with any of the king lists of Mesopotamia or Canaan. So who was this Chedorlaomer? Did he even exist? Elam was the location of the Awan I dynasty that ruled in Sumer after the fall of Ur III in 1912 BC. According to some of the Sumerian king lists, the last king of Awan I dynasty was **Kutur-Lagamar** who reigned from 1990 to 1954 BC. Some scholars believe that the Hebrew translation of *Kutur-Lagamar* could be pronounced *Chedorlaomer*. Historical documents from the cuneiform tablets in Sumer and Akkad show that neighboring kings were frequently called by the leaders of new dynasties to maintain order and collect taxes from other vassal states along trade routes. Therefore, the three kings mentioned in Genesis that accompanied Kutur-Lagamar to Sodom and Gomorrah were more than likely vassal kings from neighboring Sumer, Larsa and Gutian.

---

[289] Antiquities, 1.7.2, pg. 44
[290] Heb 7:1-3

Gerard Gertoux, a Biblical scholar, has published a thesis entitled *Dating the Chedorlaomer's death*[291] where he establishes an incredible chronological reconstruction of historical dates based on synchronisms of king lists and other extant documentation. He opines that Kutur-Lagamar was the Chedorlaomer of Genesis while documenting the *police action* (his term) that Genesis calls the four kings against five incidents. In his conclusion he states:

> "King Kutur-Lagamar (1990-1954), alias Chedorlaomer, has actually existed since he was the third and last king of Awan I, the only Elamite dynasty mentioned in Sumerian lists. His two main actions that have passed to posterity were the capture of Uruk's goddess (Nanaya) and the looting of the city of Sodom."

Abraham Visits Melchizedek

If the four kings against five incidents did occur, then we must take a hard look at one of the most interesting three lines in all of Sacred Scripture: the story of Abraham coming before Melchizedek, the king of Salem. This occurred right after Abraham was met by the king of Sodom in the Valley of the Kings where he was honored for his victory. Then, in what appears to be out of context in the story, we see these lines:

> *Melchizedek, king of Salem, brought out bread and wine. He was a priest of God Most High. He blessed Abram with these words: "Blessed be Abram by God Most High, the creator of heaven and earth; And blessed be God Most High, who delivered your foes into your hands. Then Abram gave him a tenth of everything.*[292]

Genesis states Melchizedek was, at the same time, *both king and priest* which was not the norm in Mesopotamia or Canaan. Many critics of

---

[291] https://mom.academia.edu/GerardGERTOUX, www.academia.edu/2642423/ Dating _the_Chedorlaomers_Death.

[292] Gen 14:18-20

the Hebrew Scriptures argue this point in an attempt to discredit the historicity of Genesis. Nonetheless, an Amarna *Letter* to his superiors in Egypt from one Edeb-Tob, king of Jerusalem some four hundred years after Melchizedek, claims that he too is a priest appointed by Salam, the god of peace, and is hence both king and priest in the same manner as Melchizedek. Melchizedek means *king of righteousness* and as Salam means *peace*, he was the king of righteousness and peace. Further, Genesis does not give him a genealogy as it does most important figures. We do not know from where he came or what happened to him. While monotheism is implied throughout Genesis, God's recorded conversations with Abraham deal mostly with his future as the father of a great nation, rather than telling Abraham that He is the "creator of heaven and earth." It is Melchisedech who first tells Abraham that **the God Most High** is the creator of heaven and earth. Many Christian theologians, both Catholic and Protestant, opine that because of the reference to his offerings of *bread and wine* that Melchizedek is either a *type* of or the real Jesus of Nazareth, the Messiah of Israel, who used this incident to bless the founder of the Hebrew nation.

Ishmael and Isaac

In the Abrahamic covenants, God promises that Abraham will be the father of a great nation. This must have stretched Abraham's faith to the limit as he was 87 years old (44 in my formula) and had no children by Sarah. Maybe this was the reason that Sarah offered her maidservant Hagar to her husband to father a child. Even though I posit that Abraham was a man of great intelligence, he evidently did not understand women if he thought this were not going to cause turmoil in his family. And it certainly did cause turmoil since Sarah drove the pregnant Hagar out into the desert to die where the Lord's messenger then told Hagar:

> *"I will make your descendants so numerous," added the Lord's angel, "that they will be too many to count." Then the Lord's angel said to her: "You are now pregnant and shall bear a son; and shall name him Ishmael, for the Lord has heeded your affliction.*[293]

---

[293] Gen 16:10-11

When God tells Abraham of the covenant of circumcision, he also tells him that Sarah will have a child who will be his heir. Abraham is thankful to God for this blessing, but then questions God about his beloved son Ishmael.[294] God replies:

> *Now as for Ishmael, I will heed you: I hereby bless him. I will make him fertile and will multiply him exceedingly. He shall become the father of twelve chieftains, and I will make of him a great nation. But, my covenant will remain with Isaac, whom Sarah shall bear to you by this time next year.* [295]

It is said that Ishmael is the father of the Arab nation. When Mohammed captured Arabia in 620 AD he used this passage from Genesis to claim that the Arabs were God's people and then established Islam as a religion. Notwithstanding the animosity of Islam with the Jews and Christians today, we cannot overlook this passage from Genesis. God blessed the Arabs just as He blessed the Jews even though it is clear that the Jews would be His chosen people.

The Qur'an has a lot to say about the Patriarch Abraham most of which speaks of his early life in Ur. Much of what Mohammad says is taken from what he called *the Book* (Hebrew Scriptures). The Qur'an says that Abraham argues with his father Terah about his idol worship and even destroys some of the idols.[296] After much arguing, Abraham finally chastises his own father. Mohammed also claims that Abraham tried to convince his peers that there was but one God which is reminiscent of the Hebrew tradition spoken of by Josephus. There is even a passage that describes when Abraham becomes a Moslem, which would imply that Islam was always the will of Allah.[297] While Isaac is mentioned as the son of Abraham and

---

[294] Ishmael: Translated literally it means *God has hearkened*, suggesting that a child so named was regarded as the fulfillment of a divine promise. *Encyclopedia of Religion*. Macmillan Reference USA. pp. 4551–4552.

[295] Gen 17:20-21

[296] See Biblical stories in the Qur'an, Section VI, Nr. 10, *Abraham renounces his father* http://www.answering-islam.org/Index/Stories/abraham.htm

[297] Ibid, Nr. 20 *Abraham summoned to become a Muslim*

Sarah, there is great credence given in the Qur'an to the fact that Ishmael, (note the "el" ending of the name) was Abraham's first and favorite son. In chapter 22 of Genesis, Abraham agrees to sacrifice his son Isaac at the direction of God's messenger. There is a similar story in the Qur'an except that it just says Abraham offered his son but did not say which one -- the implication being that he offered Ishmael rather than Isaac.[298]

After Abraham took Ishmael into his family, God appeared to Abraham *by the terebinth of Mamre* and later that day three visitors came to Abraham's tent with some good news. Abraham welcomed the three visitors, who told Abraham that by this same time next year his wife Sarah will give him a son. Sarah laughed at the suggestion, but Isaac was born the following year.[299]

Sodom and Gomorrah

True to their promise, two of the three men did return to visit Abraham the following year, and Abraham took them with him to the city of Sodom where he was to visit Lot. God was very upset with the actions of the people of Sodom and nearby Gomorrah and told Abraham that He was going to destroy the cities with *fire and brimstone*. Abraham argued with God that He should not *sweep away the innocent with the guilty*[300]. After a long dissertation, Abraham realized that God would destroy the cities so Abraham then returned home. The two *angels* with Abraham then entered the city of Sodom and came to the house of Lot, who welcomed them. Shortly after, the men of Sodom came to Lot's house and demanded that he give them the two visitors so that they could have *intimacies with them*.[301] Lot said the men were his guests so he could not do so – even offering his virgin daughters in their place. The men of Sodom tried to force their way into Lot's house, but the *angels* created *a blinding light so that they were utterly unable to reach the doorway*.[302] God then destroyed the cities of Sodom and Gomorrah.

---

[298] Ibid, Nr. 24, *Abraham sacrifices his son*

[299] Gen 18:1-15

[300] Gen 18:16-33

[301] Gen 19:4, Secularists today argue that God destroyed Sodom and Gomorrah, not because of the abomination of the actions of the men of Sodom, but because they did not offer hospitality.

[302] Gen 19: 11

The Kofels Event

While on the subject of the destruction of Sodom and Gomorrah, secular science may have proven an event within Genesis that had been considered a fable. This discovery also ties in with our theory that Abraham may have been an astronomer. One of the tablets from the palace of Ashurbanipal, translated by Henry Layard in the 1850's, was a copy of an ancient Sumerian astronomer's account of a "white stone bowl" approaching the earth that "vigorously swept along the sky." The tablet had been copied from the original Sumerian per Ashurbanipal's directive. Half of the tablet, known as the *Planisphere tablet* is decipherable and contained a map of the constellations in the sky at the time the tablet was written. Within the tablet the author has written notes in cuneiform giving a detailed description of the path of an object crossing the sky. Scientists have said that for a heavenly object to be seen as described on the table, the object could have been up to a kilometer in size. There was no other tablet like this in the palace library, and the *Planisphere* baffled Assyriologists and astronomers for over 150 years. Finally Mark Hempsell, an astronomer and astrophysics specialist for the British Aerospace Division, and Alan Bonds, a rocket scientist, claimed to have deciphered the tablet in their book *A Sumerian Observation of the Kofels Impact Event.*[303]

Today several computer models can replicate a star pattern from any place on earth and track it back into time so that astronomers can find the same star pattern as far back as 4000 BC with great accuracy. Bond and Hempsell used these models to calculate the night sky described on the *Planisphere* and determined that there were ten close matches from the Cancer, Gemini, Taurus sections on the *Planisphere* and notes on the tablet. The closest match was three dates of 29 June 3123, 29 June 2222 and 6 July 2269 BC. They chose the earlier date of 3123 BC as it had the most planetary and constellation matches. Right about this time in Sumerian history their epics have Enlil replacing the god Anu and goddesses Ki in the pantheon and recreating the Universe. If the heavenly body described in the *Planisphere* tablet was a large asteroid or comet, it would have caused the earth to suffer cataclysmic change that would account for a major change in the pantheon in Sumer.

---

[303] Alan Bond, Mark Hempsell *"A Sumerian Observation of the Kofels event"*, (Great Britain, Alcuin Academics Publishing, 2008, Revised), Hereafter Bond/Hempsell

Hempsell and Bond then searched for a catastrophic earth event at or near this time and found that there may have been an asteroid or comet explosive event at the small Alpine village in Switzerland named Kofels. Their theory was not without dissent within the scientific community. The fact that there was no impact crater has caused considerable skepticism with fellow scientists on the Kofels event being the result of an asteroid let alone one observed five thousand years ago by the Sumerians. Bonds and Hempsell point out that there is evidence of a massive rock slide with geological evidence of extreme heat that melted the rocks together at some time in Kofels past. There is also evidence that an object clipped off a circular section of the top of Mount Gamskogel which is on a path from the Mediterranean Sea to Kofels. Hempsell and Allan opine the impact of the heavenly object at Gamskogel caused a massive explosion in lieu of a crater, causing the rocks on Kofels to melt.

The written observation on the *Planisphere* indicated the heavenly object entered into the earth's atmosphere at a slight angle meaning it ran parallel to the earth for some time before entry into the atmosphere. The Sumerian astronomers' account would take the path of the Kofels asteroid directly up the Red Sea along the present Suez Canal across the Mediterranean along the west coast of the Adriatic Sea into the Swiss Alps at Kofels. There are pottery shards in the small town of Hvar in today's Croatia that describe the event including the *plume* that followed the asteroid. Astronomers learned from observing the impact of Comet *Sheomaker-Levey* into Jupiter in July of 1994, that objects entering a planet's atmosphere cause a *plume* of massive energy to reenter the atmosphere at or near the point of entry causing up to 70% of the asteroid to be deposited at this point in the path of the asteroid. Hempsell/Bond state in their book:

> "The rough modeling of the plume suggests the reentry would be over the Levant[304], Sinai and northern Egypt reaching into modern Syria."[305]

---

[304] The Levant is a geographic and cultural region consisting of the eastern Mediterranean between Anatolia and Egypt". The Levant today consists of Cyprus, Lebanon, Syria, the Palestinian territories, Jordan, Israel, part of southern Turkey. (Wikipedia)

[305] Bond/Hempsell, pg. 78

This puts the location of the Kofels *plume* right over Sodom and Gomorrah. Anything in that plume would have been incinerated by the incredible heat generated by the explosion of the plume and the friction upon entry which Hempsell/Bond state:

> "This would be sufficient to cause conflagration of any exposed combustible material, including people."[306]

Hempsell and Bonds also state that that what could have been the Kofels event was described in various myths and legends and could have been the cause of the destruction of Sodom and Gomorrah.

Dr. John Lewis, of NASA Space Engineering Center at the University of Arizona in his book *Rain of Fire and Ice: The Very Real Threat of Comet and Asteroid Bombardment*[307] believe that the destruction of Sodom and Gomorrah could have been caused by a comet or asteroid strike. Genesis says the following about the destruction of Sodom and Gomorrah:

> ***The Lord rained down sulfur upon Sodom and Gomorrah, fire from the Lord out of Heaven. He overthrew those cities and the whole Plain together with the inhabitants of the city and the produce of the soil. ... ... As he looked down toward Sodom and Gomorrah and the whole region of the Plain, he saw smoke over the land rising like smoke from a kiln***[308]

Lewis points out that *brimstone* is burning sulfur and fire raining down from heaven and could describe the pieces of a disintegrating heavenly body. The atmospheric impact of what scientists believe was an asteroid or comet at Tunguska, Siberia in 1908, left *sulfur* deposits and what could be described as *fire and brimstone* having come out of the sky.

---

[306] Ibid, pg. 79

[307] John Lewis, PhD, *"Rain of Fire and Ice: The Very Real Threat of comet and Asteroid Bombardment"*, (1996 Revised in 2008)

[308] Gen 19:24-25,28

Archeologists have found two ancient cities near the bottom part of the Dead Sea that they speculate could be Sodom and Gomorrah. Both cities showed signs that they were destroyed by fire. If Sodom and Gomorrah were destroyed hundreds or even a thousand years before Abraham entered Canaan, how could these two cities exist at the time of the *four kings against five* incidents in Genesis?[309] If these cities were on a trade route from Babylon to Egypt at this time in history, they certainly would have been important enough to be rebuilt.

The Planisphere tablet must have been important to the followers of the moon god Sin to be discovered and copied by Ashurbanipal fifteen hundred years later. It would seem probable that the Sumerians also wrote of the cataclysmic event that followed the asteroid impact, which would have blotted out the sun for some time although, to date, we have not discovered any such record. Abraham, as a literate devotee of Sin in Ur III, could have had knowledge of the tablet and brought this with him into Canaan. Certainly the people in the Levant would have recalled the destruction of Sodom and Gomorrah and kept it in their lore. The *Planisphere tablet* and the *Kofels event* are evidence that the worshipers of the moon god Sin in Akkad were highly proficient in astronomy as far back as the third and maybe even the fourth millennium BC.

Abraham's Last Years

Sarah died in Hebron at the age of 127. Abraham purchased a plot of land for her burial from the Hittites, who evidently controlled Hebron at this time in history. The Hittites offered the land to Abraham without charge, but Abraham insisted on purchasing the land for four hundred shekels of silver with a formal bill of sale as was the custom in his homeland.[310] This purchase is one of the current Israelis' claims that their ancestors purchased the land of Canaan and therefore have a right to it this day.

The first five versus of Chapter 25 in Genesis are very interesting. It states that after Sarah died, Abraham **married another wife, whose name was Keturah** who bore him five sons whose genealogy is listed. The interesting part of this narrative is that Keturah is listed as Abraham's wife not his

---

[309] Gen 14:9
[310] Gen 23:1-16

concubine. As a wife, her children would be in a line of succession after Isaac to Abraham's estate. Yet, we find little information about these five heirs. Notwithstanding the words of Genesis, Jewish tradition is that Keturah was a concubine, which would seem to be substantiated here:

> **Abraham gave everything that he owned to his son Isaac. To the sons of his concubinage, however, he made grants while he was still living, as he sent them away eastward, to the land of Kedem, away from his son Isaac.**[311]

From what we have learned about Abraham's culture in Ur III, we can assume that there was a written will signed by Abraham for this decree as this was the practice in Ur III at the time of Abraham as shown by the thousands of similar legal tablets. If Abraham wrote the will on fire hardened tablets in cuneiform, maybe someday it will be found.

Abraham died at the ripe old age of 175 and was buried by his sons Ismael and Isaac in the same *cave of Machpelah in the field of Ephron* that he had purchased for Sarah. There is no better way to describe the life of Abraham other than what Melchizedek, king of Salem said of him:

> **Blessed be Abram by God Most High**[312]

And God did bless Abraham, the son of Terah. His descendants *are as numerous as the stars in the sky* for he is still called *Our Father Abraham* by over half of all the people on the earth today.

---

[311] Gen 25:5-6
[312] Gen 14:19

CHAPTER ELEVEN

AFTER ABRAHAM

There God, speaking to Israel in a vision by night, called: Jacob! Jacob! He answered, "Here I am." Then he said: I am God, the God of your father. Do not be afraid to go down to Egypt, for there I will make you a great nation. I will go down to Egypt with you I will also bring you back here, after Joseph has closed your eyes.[313]

Secular history sheds some very interesting facts on the fate of Abraham's family during their time in Egypt. Abraham's grandson Jacob, who God will rename Israel, and his twelve sons will go to Egypt as a result of famine in Canaan. According to the Seder Olan, Joseph was sold into slavery into Egypt in 1708 BC[314]; and because of his great skills was put in charge of distributing the Pharaoh's grain.[315] By this time, the Hyksos had established complete control of the Nile Delta as we see from the timeline established in Gertoux's paper on *Dating the war of the time of the Hyksos*:

---

[313] Gen: 46:2-4

[314] Gen 37:28 "They sold Joseph to the Ishmaelites for twenty pieces of silver." One wonders if these were Abraham's own grandchildren from Ishmael. If so, maybe they too will become Hyksos.

[315] Gen 41: 56-57

"The three Hyksos dynasties (XIV, XV, and XVI) ruled
Egypt approximately from 1750 to 1530 BCE"[316]

This puts Joseph into an Egypt controlled by Semites forty-two years after
the Hyksos gained control of the upper Nile delta. After all, Joseph was a
Semite just as the Hyksos. Josephus in his discussion of the Hyksos kings
refers to this fact when he says:

"Since one of our ancestors, Joseph, told the king of Egypt
that he was a 'captive', and afterwards sent for his brethren
into Egypt by the king's permission."[317]

Regardless of when Abraham left Haran, it is quite probable that Joseph
would have been sold into slavery in Egypt during the Hyksos period.
This gives us the relatively short chronology of the Hyksos period (1750-
1530 B.C.) to backdate with some historical certainty the time of the
Patriarchs in Canaan. If Joseph came into Hyksos Egypt and was later
joined by his extended family of eleven brothers, they would have grown
to become the Hebrew nation by the time the Hyksos were discharged
by the Egyptians in 1530 BC. This would account for the change of the
Hebrews from a thriving nation friendly with Pharaoh to one in slavery.
When the Egyptians defeated a people, they killed the royalty and military
leaders, taking the majority of the people as slaves (booty). As we see in
the book of Exodus:

**Then a new king, who knew nothing of Joseph, rose to
power in Egypt**[318]

Under the Gertoux timeline, the Hebrews would have been slaves from
1530 to 1476 BC, which is when the Exodus occurred and is enough
time for God to direct Moses to tell Pharaoh to **set my people free**.
Gertoux' paper goes into extensive detail of Egyptian history and opines
that the Hyksos king Apopi, one of the last Hyksos leaders, could well have
been Moses. There is little to substantiate such an interesting hypothesis,

---

[316] Gertoux/Hyksos, pg. 1

[317] Josephus, Against Apion, 1.14.92, and pg. 933 – "*Captive*" was another name for
Shepherds in the story.

[318] Ex 1:8

although Exodus does give Moses a royal family background, and he was certainly known enough by Pharaoh to be allowed to ask for the freedom of his people. The reason I give such high regard for the Gertoux timeline is the highly documented research that he uses in his *ancient chorological system* of study. His work equates the Hebrews with the Hyksos with some certainty.

The Hyksos city of Avaris is of interest because its location makes some believe that it could be the Biblical Goshen. Avaris was abandoned after the Hyksos were driven out in 1530 BC, after an eighteen-year campaign by Ahmose I. Avaris was then used as a site for very large silos for storage of grain for the off years of food production. One wonders if those granaries were the ones suggested by Joseph to Pharaoh to use in the ***seven years of great abundance to prepare for the seven years of famine.***[319] Josephus quotes the historian Manetho that the eighteen-year siege could not win the battle, leading to a negotiated settlement allowing the Asiatics to return peacefully to Canaan – which is exactly what Moses did in Exodus although with some embellishments. Manetho's claim has some scholars wondering if this was not the basis of the Exodus itself.

Disputed Date of the Exodus

The date of the Exodus is still in question. The Seder Olam states the Israelites left in mass to Canaan in 1476 BC (as does Josephus), while some Biblical scholars opine the later date of 1250 BC during the time of Ramses II. There are several references within the Amarna Letters (1388-1332 BC) to the "*Habiru* (also translated *Habiri*)" which many scholars, but certainly not all, believe are the Hebrews. A Biblical scholar reading these letters would be hard pressed not to believe that they refer to the Hebrews during the time of Joshua. In 1920, Percy Handcock published a book showing the translations of the Amarna Letters.[320] While fascinating to read, they are as practical as any government official of today writing to his head of state. The letters show that by the middle of the thirteenth century BC,

---

[319] Gen 41:25-43

[320] Percy Handcock, M.A., *Selections from the Tell El-Amarna Letters*, ed. Skeel, White, Whitney (London, MacMillan Co., 1920) (Hereafter, Handcock/ Amarna Letters)

Egypt had garrisons in southern Canaan but that their influence was waning evidently due to the interference of the Habiru. There are several letters from Abdi-hiba, the governor of Jerusalem, telling the Egyptian king to send troops, or he will lose more ground in Canaan due to the interference of the Habiru. We see one letter from Abdi-hiba to the king that the Habiru are a threat all around him:

> "But now the Habiru hold the cities of the king. There is no local ruler left to the king, my lord; all are lost. Behold, Turbazu has been slain in the gate of Zilft; yet the king does nothing. Behold, Zimrida of Lachish, his servants have slaughtered him ... The Habiru, Behold the land of Grinti-kirmil belongs to Tagi, and the people of Ginti form a garrison in Betsani; and the same will befall us now that Labaya and the land of Shakmi have given everything to the Habiru ..." [321]

The Amarna Letters also refer to a war in the north of Canaan involving the Habiru against a confederation of Japhia king of Gezer, Jabin king of Hazor and Adonizedek king of Jerusalem -- all of whom chapter 11 of Joshua says were defeated by the Hebrews shortly after entering Canaan.

The argument against the Habiru of the Amarna Letters being the Hebrews is that the book of Exodus clearly states:

> **_The time the Israelites had stayed in Egypt was four hundred and thirty years._[322]**

According to Gertoux, "Jewish translators of the Septuagint were aware of this ambiguity and thus choose to add an interpolation in order to prevent any misunderstanding: "land of Egypt [and in the land of Canaan] was four hundred and thirty years long."[323] Further, Exodus states the Israelis were put to labor in the cities of Pithom and Raamses. Some Biblical scholars believe Raamses was Pi-Ramsses, built by Ramesses II, who lived

---

[321] Ibid, pg. 9

[322] Ex 12:40

[323] Gertoux/Hyksos

in the 12th century BC,[324] which matches the 430 years stated above. However, in the same Hebrew Scriptures, chapter six of 1 Kings says:

> *In the four hundred and eightieth years from the departure of the Israelites from the land of Egypt, in the fourth year of Solomon's reign over Israel -- the construction of the temple was begun.*[325]

Most Biblical scholars place the fourth year of Solomon's reign at 1010 BC, placing the Exodus in 1490 BC, and putting the Israelites across the Jordan in 1450 BC. Meanwhile, Josephus claims in *Antiquities:*

> "Four hundred and thirty years after our forefather Abraham came into Canaan, but two hundred and fifteen years only after Jacob removed into Egypt"[326]

If Josephus is correct, this would mark the time of the Exodus of the Hebrews into Canaan in 1476 BC, the time of Kings Japhia, Jabin and Adonizedik. The Seder Olam timeline also claims, "The Israelites left in a mass exodus from Egypt in 1476 BC."

As we observed when we analyzed *Who wrote the Bible* there is a strong possibility that the Hebrews' four hundred years in Egypt, as written in Exodus 12, could well have been a scribal error or erroneous interpretation of facts, which we know were frequent. Whatever the case, secular history seems to confirm the dates of I Kings and the Seder Olam. Biblical scholars who adhere to a literal translation of Scripture find it hard to accept the view of Josephus and the Jewish tradition on this subject even when confronted with the I Kings date.

---

[324] Egyptian: alternatively transcribed as Rameses and Ramses referred to as Ramesses the Great, was the third Egyptian pharaoh (reigned 1279 BC – 1213 BC) of the Nineteenth dynasty. He is often regarded as the greatest, most celebrated, and most powerful pharaoh of the Egyptian Empire. His successors and later Egyptians called him the *Great Ancestor*. Ramesses II led several military expeditions into the Levant, reasserting Egyptian control over Canaan. Wikipedia.

[325] I Kgs:6:1

[326] Antiquities 2.15.2, pg. 87

The ***Stele of Merneptah,***[327] which is now located in the Cairo Museum, was crafted in Egypt in 1209 BC, to celebrate the victories of the Pharaoh Merneptah over the Canaanites. It states: "Israel is laid waste, its seed is not." It would appear then the Israelis were in Canaan by at least the twelfth century BC. It is hard to believe that if the Hebrews arrived in Canaan a few years earlier, as Exodus 12 tells us, that the Israelis would be known as a separate race in Canaan at the time of the Merneptan stele. I personally believe the Exodus occurred in 1476 BC.

The Amarna Letters also reveal the Canaanites to have a more advanced civilization at the time of the Patriarchs than originally thought. It is of interest to linguists that many Canaanite words in the Amarna Letters are almost identical to the same words in Hebrew and to those used in Palestine today. The Tell el-Amarna Letters give us credible information that Canaan may have been more diverse than had been thought at the time that Abraham traveled there, and probably had a Babylonian and Egyptian influence in its politics. If the Babylonians had an early presence in Canaan, then Abraham might well have been a part of a major migration of Semites from Mesopotamia into Canaan. The history of the Hyksos, the Amarna Letters and the Merneptan stele are the most serious finds to date that approximate an extra- Biblical record of the Exodus.

---

[327] Discovered in 1896, the Merneptah Stele is a seven foot slab of black granite found in a temple in Thebes. Pharaoh Merneptah was the son of Ramses the Great.

Chapter Twelve

Connecting the Dots

"Data! Data! Data!" he cried impatiently. "I can't make bricks without clay." Sherlock Holmes -The Adventure of the Copper Beeches[328]

We have reviewed in detail those parts of Genesis dealing with the patriarch Abraham, and we have introduced secular historical data that deal with the same subject. Each of these details is a dot in the picture of the landscape depicting the life of Abraham. As Sherlock Holmes implied above, it is time to connect the dots to see if we can come to some conclusions.

First, let us return to the original question of this study. Did Terah and Abraham exist in ancient Mesopotamia? I am convinced that the study of historical Mesopotamia gives credibility to the Biblical Abraham in Mesopotamia and Canaan. The unstable political atmosphere in Ur III in 2000 BC was certainly conducive to a mass exodus from *Ur of the Chaldees* north to other lands. The fact that Haran was a familiar destination for a worshiper of the moon god Sin by Terah and his family gives reasonable explanation why the family chose Haran as a destination after leaving the city of Ur. Our study of the culture of Ur III at the time that Terah lived there would make me believe that his society was highly advanced, that his family was wealthy and probably of landowning gentry stock,

---

[328] *The Adventures of Sherlock Holmes*, Sir Arthur Conon Doyle. First published in Strand Magazine in June 1892.

which would make our Abraham literate and most likely well-educated. From what we know of Ur III, it is quite likely that Abraham was a well-accomplished man of his time, and his family had accumulated a large amount of property and slaves. This is an important fact to consider as we see his life unfold.

Climatologists' discovery of a major drought in upper Mesopotamia in 2200 BC, and the entry of the Hyksos into Egypt shortly after, lead me to believe there was a major Mesopotamian immigration into the Levant of Canaan and eventually into Egypt about the time that Abraham and his family migrated into Canaan. The Scriptural reason for Abraham's entering Canaan was to follow the will of God, yet as we see every day, God's will is frequently fulfilled in the otherwise normal events of world history. The various references to Abraham as a warrior in the Genesis story makes me believe that he could well have been an appointed leader of an expedition into Canaan on one of these migrations. How else would he have credentials to meet the Pharaoh? The Amarna Letters also prove that this migration of Semites from Assyria was well-established in Canaan as early as 1460 BC, which I believe was about the time that Abraham's progeny were returning to Canaan from Egypt to claim the land that God had promised to Abraham.

Revelation and History

The relationship of ancient Semitic epics to the stories in Genesis is clear from this study. As a citizen of the Third Dynasty of Ur, Terah and his sons were exposed to the world's most literate civilization. Archeologists have found remains of academies called *edubbas* in Mesopotamia where students were taught to read and write using the ancient myths and stories as textbooks. They also found tablets written by students with corrections by the scribe. Therefore, it seems logical that Terah and Abraham, as property owners in Ur III, would have been well-versed in these ancient stories, myths, and poems and also literate.

As we have seen by the small size of the Tell el-Amarna tablets, Akkadian cuneiform documents of Abraham's time could hold considerable information on very small and easily transportable clay tablets. One estimate is that the total information transferred on the 382 Amarna tablets is equal to about half of the words in the first five books of the Hebrew Scriptures. Noel Kramer found a cuneiform *catalogue tablet* from Nippur 2½ x by 1½ inches that contained a catalogue of the titles of sixty-two Sumerian literary compositions.[329] Abraham could easily have copied and carried with him the entire lot of ancient Mesopotamian stories to be kept by his descendants and read by Moses. If my theory is correct, Abraham was one of history's greatest historians of ancient Mesopotamian lore as his stories have survived for four thousand years and are incorporated in the world's most printed and distributed book in history: the Bible.

It is clear to well-read Christians and Jews that not all of these ancient stories impart a theological lesson as the parallel story does in Genesis. That is the genius of the author who was inspired by the Holy Spirit to use these stories to give us knowledge of God and His will. But, as Jesus of Nazareth did two thousand years later with the use of parables, a good story can be used to impart a moral behavior that the original story did not intend. Just because there are Genesis-like stories in ancient literature that does not mean that the Hebrews obtained their theology from a pagan religion. That being said, many of our current concepts of deity, spiritual beings, heaven and hell may have been inspired and derived from the earlier writings of ancient Sumer and Akkad. Some will be disturbed by this fact because the Sumerians and Akkadians were polytheists; still, as we have shown, Abraham more than likely worshiped other gods before God called him to lead the world towards the monotheism that we know today.

With the experience of twenty-five hundred years of a developed monotheism, we look at polytheism as pagan, somehow evil and anarchic; however, that does not mean that the people of Abraham's time were not God-fearing or intelligent. They certainly were not atheists. The societies of ancient Mesopotamia had a highly complex concept of deity and brought these concepts to us in history's earliest known written literary achievements. Their epics show their theologies developed instinctively and were a step in God's Plan of Salvation. Like our secular brothers and sisters of today, they were just looking for God in all the wrong places.

I believe God determined that mankind was advanced enough at the time of Abraham to accept His revelation that there was but one creating God.

---

[329] Kramer/History, pg. 16

As we have seen, it will only be the first step towards the monotheism that we practice today. Whether Abraham had developed our understanding of monotheism during his lifetime is arguable, and neither secular history nor Genesis can help us discern the truth. As we see in the Near Eastern testimony handed down to us, while polytheism did evolve into a concept of one superior god at the head of the pantheon, it retained the ancient belief in many gods and was still anthropomorphic. Mythical polytheism was man's invention, and until man learned otherwise it would remain the principal form of deity worship worldwide for another two thousand years, and is still practiced in one fifth of the world's population today.

Did Abraham Worship Other Gods?

Jewish tradition, as outlined in the Seder Olam, has Abraham born 1948 years after Creation in Genesis (1976 BC). Hebrew Scripture and Jewish tradition then assume that all men of this time were aware of and worshiped the God revealed to Adam and Eve and Noah. Early Genesis follows the patriarchs through Noah, who the Seder Olam says died 58 years after Abraham was born. Orthodox Jews and some Evangelical Christians who interpret the Hebrew Scriptures literally share this belief. If one follows this tradition, Abraham would have understood the creating God of early Genesis and his life experience in Ur would not be paramount to our study. On the other hand, if we incorporate the secular history of Mesopotamia and Canaan into the life of Abraham, we find polytheism as the predominant religious viewpoint and not the monotheism that is implied in early Genesis. The Hebrew Scriptures do not tell us that Abraham "served other gods" as it does about his father Terah. However, it would be logical to assume that the historical Abraham was no different from any other citizen of the Third Dynasty of Ur in 2000 BC, and would have been raised a polytheist just like his father. This being said, it does not mean that Abraham did not argue a one God of creation theology even if it would have been an anathema to his peers. The Hebrew tradition, in the Talmud and by Josephus as well as that of the Qur'an, is that Abraham developed an aversion to polytheism and argued with his fellows that there was but one God who created the universe. As we read in Josephus earlier, Abraham was possibly educated in astronomy as part of his moon god worship of astrology. It is quite possible that the men in his academic circles were privately skeptical of any kind of deity, much like our scientists of today. These are the men that brought us advanced mathematics including the concept of the 360 degree circle, and who some astronomers believe had determined the circumference of the earth from formula and observation alone. If Josephus was right, Abraham and his peers were true academics and highly intelligent; therefore, there may have been discussions within his circle of friends on this subject of one creating God from scientific deduction, if not revelation. However, their society was not as tolerant of such free thinking as ours, and such talk would have been treasonous, considering the fact that temple priests, who were highly political, controlled the observatories. For that reason any such opinions would not likely be published. On the other hand, considering the explosion of archeological finds in the Near East recently[330], maybe archeologists will someday find ancient tablets in Ur or Haran giving us evidence of such thinking.

Genesis was written at a time when the Jews understood that Yahweh was the God of the Hebrews and the only God that created the universe. In my opinion, the redactor of the Hebrew Scriptures projected this post-Sinai belief back to the time of Abraham in Genesis. This brings up an interesting point that is discussed in a blog on a Jewish website[331] that asks: *Was Abraham truly a Jew?* The author posits that because Abraham lived well before the Exodus wherein God gave Moses the Torah at Sinai, he could not have been required to abide by the laws of Judaism and was therefore not really a Jew. I believe this discussion exposes a reality about Abraham. As he had not yet received the truth of the Torah, he was not fully required to believe in a single God that created the Universe. To the people of Abraham's time, the closest concept of a creating god was the many ancient deities of Sumer, Akkad and Canaan in their many epics.

God's revelations to Abraham would have been incredulous to an educated polytheist of his day – even a polytheism which had evolved into monolatry with a supreme god in the pantheon. Yet, God did reveal Himself and Abraham believed and maintained his faith in the words of this God who

---

[330] During the year and half I have researched this work, there have been three major archeological finds that enhance our understanding of the Hebrew Scriptures. These finds are footnoted earlier.

[331] The article was titled: *Did the Chosen Nation Start with Abraham.* I have been unable to retrace the source website.

appeared to him. It is for this faith that he is credited as being *righteous --* righteous in the eyes of God as Abraham believed *God would make of him a great nation*. This is shown best in the words of one of Abraham's descendants, Paul of Tarsus, who in his classic dissertation on *faith* in the letter to the Romans said it best:

> *What then can we say that Abraham found, our ancestor according to the flesh? Indeed, if Abraham was justified on the basis of his works, he has reason to boast; but this was not so in the sight of God. For what does the Scripture say? "Abraham believed God, and it was credited to him as righteousness."*[332]

In the Abrahamic Covenant God asked Abraham to establish the Hebrew nation and in exchange He will be their God. Both sides kept the promise.

Abrahams Role in God's Plan of Salvation

It is the thesis of this book that God's first step in the development of monotheism was to reveal Himself to Abraham and charge him with the duty to develop a distinct race of people – the Hebrews. In exchange, God will be that people's deity and protectorate – much as the gods of Mesopotamia were for city-states and empires. Abraham was to believe and love this God, and in exchange this God would build Abraham's descendants into a unique and special race of people that will continue God's Plan of Salvation. Abraham's immediate descendants knew of this *God of Abraham;* and they took this knowledge with them when they immigrated into Egypt during the time of Joseph, where they eventually became slaves, probably when the Hyksos were expelled by the Egyptians. Eventually God chose another Hebrew named Moses to bring His people out of Egypt into the land promised to Abraham. By this time, the Hebrew nation was numbered in the hundreds of thousands (some scholars say millions) and was a force to be reckoned with in Canaan as seen in the Amarna Letters. Moses was also directed by God's personal call to catechize his people before they returned to Canaan, and he did so for forty years while they sojourned in the desert. Finally on Mount Sinai, God gave the

---

[332] Rom 4: 1-4

Law to His people, and they possessed a formalized religion to accept or reject. In this Law they were told to love this God above all others and that there was no other God, which established a clear choice between the polytheism of the world around them and the monotheism God wanted his people to embrace. It was the Hebrews under the direction of *the God of Abraham* that affected this major theological paradigm shift. C. S. Lewis may have said it best in *Mere Christianity* when he talked about God's use of the Jews:

> "He (God) selected one particular people and spent centuries hammering into their heads the sort of God He was – that there was only one of Him and that He cared about right conduct. These people were the Jews, and the Old Testament gives an account of the hammering process."[333]

And a major change it was. The idea that there was only one God who created everything was unique within the known world. The Greeks and Romans continued polytheism until the fourth century AD. At that time it was replaced within the Roman Empire with the teachings of a descendant of Abraham, one named Jesus from Nazareth in Galilee.

Authors Final Statement

I believe in the revelations of God to Abraham as stated in the Hebrew Scriptures and at the same time recognize the truth of secular history. There was an historical Abraham, and God did reveal Himself to this man two thousand years before He Himself will be presented to mankind through His Son. God must have been proud of this man that He chose to usher in the first stages of monotheism to the world. Certainly all Jews, Christians and Moslems share that pride.

---

[333] C.S. Lewis, Mere Christianity, (New York, Harper press, 1952), pg. 50

ACKNOWLEDGEMENTS

I am not sure what motivated me to write this book as I am a retired insurance guy, not an author. I do know that a voice was speaking to me almost every morning at mass for months, telling me to write the story of Abraham. As I have always loved history, when I started to research the patriarch of our religion it became clear to me I had to show the influence of ancient Mesopotamia on the word of God in the Hebrew Scriptures. Every time I discovered a connection to secular history and the Hebrew Scriptures, I would yell to my wife Dorothy: "you won't believe what I just found." Her fain of interest must have tested her patience over the year and half I worked on this book.

The seed of this story came from the seven year Bible Study conducted by Dr. Bill Creasy of Logos Ministries at our Mission Basilica Parish in San Juan Capistrano, California. Dr. Bill's lectures were a life changer for me and Dorothy. Dr. Creasy taught the Bible as a literary work at UCLA before retiring to dedicate his life to spreading the Gospel. In class he read the Bible out-loud from the first word of Genesis to the last word of Revelation, making even the book of Numbers interesting. His side-track emphasis on how geography and history affected each story was the motivating factor in my research into the secular history at the time of Abraham in this book. Without Bill's gift of making the Bible come to life, I would never have come to know the Word of God to its fullest. When he led our class to Israel and read the words of Our Lord at the same spot where they were spoken two thousand years ago, I could feel the realism of my Christian faith.

I would like to thank Father John Bradley, my grammar editor, whose work solved one of the mysteries of my life. For years I have wondered why Sister

Mary Erna of St. Augustine Parish School in Des Moines had me write "I will not talk in class" on the blackboard one hundred times. I now realize I must have been talking when she was teaching us how to use a comma and a semi-colon. If the reader finds any errors in grammar, it is not Father John's fault but mine on rewrites after his editing.

I would also like to thank the guys in my *morning-mass coffee group* who found me a heretic more than once when I was explaining my theories in this book. Their patience in listening to my balderdash was certainly the result of the graces they had just received.

It is very seldom that a father admits that he learned something from his son. But in my case, in a roundabout way that is what happened several years ago on our annual fishing trip to Alaska. One night after dinner at Redoubt Mountain Lodge on Crescent Lake, we were discussing the Incarnation. He asked why God chose the tiny country of Israel over the highly advanced cultures of China or India to send His son to mankind. Even with my Miller Light induced keen insight, I found I could not answer the question to his or my satisfaction. I must admit that this question has haunted me ever since. Little did I know at the time that this question is known by theologians as *The Scandal of Particularity* and has been asked by theologians for centuries. Fortunately I think I have answered it, at least to my satisfaction, at the end of this book when I give my theories as to what part Abraham played in God's plan of salvation. So, I must thank my son Paul for spicing my life with this riddle that had so much to do with the writing of this book.

Finally, I must thank my partner in faith and beautiful wife, Dorothy who kept me going on this work even when I thought it was a waste of time. If there is any benefit to the readers of the book, it is her faith in me that is the credit.

BIBLIOGRAPHY

ROMAN CATHOLIC DOCUMENTS

New American Bible, 1970, Confraternity of Christian Doctrine, Wash D.C., Old Testament Imprimatur: Patrick Cardinal O'Boyle D. D. Archbishop of Washington, July 27, 1970; New Testament Imprimatur: James A. Hickey, S.T.D., J.C.D. Archbishop of Washington, August 27, 1986.

Catechism of the Catholic Church, Rev. Peter M.J. Stravinskas, Ph.D., S.T.D., Ed. English translation of the *Catechism of the Catholic Church for the United States of America.* (Ignatius Press, English translation, 1994, United States Catholic Conference, Inc.—Libreria Editrice Vaticana)

The Basic Sixteen Documents, Vatican II Constitutions, Decrees, Declarations, Austin Flannery, OP, Gen Ed. (Costello Publishing Co. Inc., Northport NY, 1996), a complete translation of all of the documents of the Second Vatican Conference which was first published in 1975.

SOURCE DOCUMENTS

Pritchard, James B. ed. *Ancient Near Eastern Texts, Relating to the Old Testament,* (New Jersey, Princeton University Press, 3rd Edition with Supplement, 1969) this book simply referred to as "Pritchard" in the academic community is considered the most complete *source document* for translations of ancient documents that deal with Hebrew Scriptures.

Arnold, Bill T. Byer, Bryan E. ed., *Readings from the Ancient near East – Primary Sources of Old Testament Study*, (Grand Rapids, Michigan, Baker

Academic, 2002) Another version of translations of ancient Mesopotamian epics and literature.

Winston, William, A.M, ed., *Josephus, the Complete Works*, (Nashville, Thomas Nelson Publisher, 1998). The complete works of the Jewish historian Flavius Josephus which he wrote for the library of Rome. We are most interested in his classic *The Antiquities of the Jews,* which along with the Talmud is considered the most complete written history of the Jews outside of Scripture.

Kramer, Samuel Noah, *Sumerian Mythology*, (Philadelphia, University of Pennsylvania Press, 1961) The book was originally published in 1944 and was a basic source document for Sumerian Epics and literature, some of which were originally translated by Kramer.

Todd M. Johnson, Ph.D., Brian J Grim, Ph.D., ed. *World Religion Database, - International religious demographic statistics and sources.* (Koninklijke Brill NV, Boston University, 2008.) The WRD contains detailed statistics on religious affiliation for every country of the world. It offers best estimates at multiple dates for each of the world's religions for the period 1900 to 2050. http://www.worldreligiondatabase.org

ANNOTATED BIBLIOGRAPHY BY AUTHOR

Bond, Alan, Hempsell, Mark, *A Sumerian Observation of the Kofels Impact Event*, (Great Britain, Alcuin Academics Publishing, Revised edition 2008), A well-documented hypothesis using ancient and current documents that may pinpoint what caused the destruction of Sodom and Gomorrah and when.

Bottero, Jean, *Everyday Life in Ancient Mesopotamia*, (Baltimore, John Hopkins Univ. Press, 1992) Bottero is a French historian and Assyriologist who wrote several books on Ancient Near East Religions including *The Birth of God* and *Everyday life in ancient Mesopotamia.*

Day, John, *Yahweh and the Gods and Goddesses of Canaan*, (Sheffield Academic Press, Ltd New York, 2002), Discusses the relationship of Yahweh to the Canaanite gods El and Ba'al.

Diakanoff, Igor Mikhailovich, *Sumer: Society and State in Ancient Mesopotamia.* (Moscow, IVL Publishers, 1959), Diakanoff's study was referenced in Kramer's book *The Sumerians.* For more on Diakanoff see www.orientalstudies.ru.

Fagan, Brian, Durrani, Nadia, *People of the earth: an introduction to world prehistory.* (Pearson Prentice Hall, 2004) A study of the history of our human past from the earliest times until man established civilized society.

Ferguson, Everett, *Backgrounds of Early Christianity* Grand Rapids, Michigan, William B. Eerdmans Publishing Company, Third ed. 2003), Textbook detailing the geopolitical world as it viewed philosophy and religion.

Finkel, Irving, *the Ark before the Noah, Decoding the Story of the Flood,* (UK, Hodder & Stoughton, 2014). Dr Irving Finkel is Assistant Keeper of Ancient Mesopotamian script, languages and cultures at the British Museum. He has discovered a missing cuneiform tablet of the Noah-Like story in an Akkadian myth.

Friedman, Richard Elliot, *Who wrote the Bible?* (New York, Harper and Row, Publishers, 1987), a discussion of the *Four Sources Theory* which opines that the Hebrew Scriptures were written by four different authors and put together by a redactor on or about 600 BC.

Friedman, Richard Elliot, *The Bible with Sources Revealed, A new view into the five books of Moses,* (New York, Harper Collins Publishers, 2003); Friedman exhibits a side by side analysis of the Hebrew Scriptures highlighting the grammatical and literary differences of four sources.

Guggenheimer, Heinrich W. ED., *Seder Olam Rabbah: The Rabbinic View of Biblical Chronology,* (Rowman and Littlefield Publishers, Inc., Lanham, Maryland, 1998). *Seder Olam* is the basic text on which historical understanding of Jewish tradition.

Hahnenberg, Edward P. *A Concise Guide to the Documents of Vatican II,* (Cincinnati, St. Anthony Messenger Press, 2007), a recent analysis of the Vatican II documents.

Kellert, Stephen H. *In the Wake of Chaos: Unpredictable Order in Dynamical Systems.* (Chicago, University of Chicago Press, 1993) A secular discussion of the Chaos of creation and today's world.

Kramer, Samuel Noah, *History begins at Sumer: Thirty-Nine Firsts in recorded history* (Philadelphia, University of Penn Press, Third revised Edition, 1981) Kramer, who was born in Russia in 1897, first went to Iraq to study the Sumerian civilization in 1930. This, one of his first books on Sumer, annotates many of the *firsts* that the Sumerians brought to the civilized world.

Kramer, Samuel Noah, *The Sumerians: Their History, Culture, and Character* (Chicago, University of Chicago Press, *1971*) Kramer brings the life of the Sumerians to us in this more detailed description of their religion, education and literature, much which he personally translated from ancient cuneiform tablets.

Leick, Gwendolyn, Mesopotamia, *The Invention of the City* (London, Penguin Books, 2001), Extensive history of Mesopotamia from the first known city-state of Eridu thru the end of the Babylon empire.

Lewis, John, PhD, *Rain of Fire and Ice: The Very Real Threat of comet and Asteroid Bombardment,* (Reading, Mass., Addison-Wesley Publishing Co., 1996 Revised in 2008), A theory that comets and asteroids have bombarded the earth in ancient times including possibly at Sodom and Gomorrah.

Robinson, Edward ed., *The Brown-Driver-Briggs Hebrew and English Lexicon: With an Appendix Containing the Biblical Aramaic:* (Peabody Mass., Hendrickson Publishers, 1906) A trio of eminent Old Testament scholars-Francis Brown, R. Driver, and Charles Briggs-spent over twenty years researching, writing, and preparing The Brown-Driver-Briggs Hebrew and English Lexicon.

Ryan, William B.R, Pitman, Walter B. *Noah's flood, The New Scientific Discoveries about the Event that Changed History* (New York, Simon & Shuster, Inc. 1998). A scientific study of the formation of the Black Sea due to collapse of the Bosporus straight in 5300 BC.

Sanders, N.K., *The Epic of Gilgamesh, an English version with an introductory* (England, Penguin Books, 1972), Sanders has given us a history of the most ancient piece of literature known to man; and a chapter by chapter analysis of the story.

Seewald, Peter, Benedict XVI, *Light of the World: The Pope, The Church and the signs of the times, A conversation with Peter Seewald,* (San Francisco, Ignatius Press, 2010, copyright by Libreria Editrice Vaticana) A discussion with Pope Emeritus Benedict XVI on the subject of the Historical Critical Method of Bible study.

Segal, Alan F., *Life after Death: a History of the Afterlife in the Religions of the West.* (New York, Doubleday, 2004) Segal uses ancient literature, history and philosophy to relate how ancient civilizations grappled with the question of an afterlife.

Smith, Mark S., *The Early History of God, Yahweh and the Other Deities in Ancient Israel*, (Grand Rapids, Michigan. William B. Eerdmans Publishing Company, Cambridge U.K., 2002) A detailed analysis of the relationship of Hebrew Scriptures and ancient Canaanite theology.

Smith, Mark S, *Origins of Biblical Monotheism, Israel's Polytheistic Background and the Ugaritic Texts*, (New York, Oxford University Press, 2001) An updated version of his *History of God* book in light of the translations of the Ugaritic literature.

Smith, Mark S. Coogan, Michael D. *Stories from Ancient Canaan*, Second Edition, (Louisville, Kentucky, John Knox Press, 2012), A detailed study of Ugaritic text as they concern Hebrew Scriptures.

Wilson Ian, *Before the Flood, The Biblical Flood as a real event and how it changed the course of civilization.* (New York, St. Martin's Press, 2001) Discusses and elaborates on the catastrophic event recently recorded by William Ryan and Walter Pitman in their book Noah's Flood.

Woolley, Leonard C., and Hall, Henry R., *Al-'Ubaid. Ur Excavations,* (Oxford, Oxford University Press, 1927) Notes on the **excavations** of 1919 at Muqayyar, **el**-cObeid, and Abu Shahrein, which is the ancient city of Ur in southern Iraq.

Wooley, Leonard C., *Ur of the Chaldees: A Revised and Updated Edition of Sir Leonard Woolley's Excavations at Ur,* P.R. S. Moorey, Ed. (Ithaca, NY, Cornell Univ. Press, 1982), an illustrated version of Woolley's classic book on his excavation of Ur.

ENCYCLOPEDIAS

Catholic Encyclopedia, *2009,* Article on *Ba'al, Ballim,* http://www.newadvent.org

Jewish Encyclopedia, 2002, Article on Sheol, www.jewishencyclopedia.com

Encyclopaedia Britannica 1961, Article on Masoretic Text.

www.britannica.com/EBchecked/topic/368081/Masoretic-text

Ancient History Encyclopedia, 2009, http://www.ancient.eu.com. Article on the Amorites.

Encyclopedia of World History: Ancient, Medieval and Modern - Chronologically Arranged, 1972, Article on Catal Huyuk civilization.

NEWPAPER AND MAGAZINE ARTICLES

Barton, George A., *Historical Value of the Patriarchal Narratives, Proceedings of the American Philosophical Society, Vol. 52, April 1,* 1913.

Welford, John Noble, *Collapse Linked to Drought*, NY Times, 24 August 1993

Sham, Sandra, *The World's First Temple.* Archaeology Magazine, Vol. 61, Nov/Dec 2008

Hershner, Isabel, *Pollen Study Points to Drought as Culprit in Bronze Age Mystery*, New York Times, 22 October, 2013.

Gibbons, Ann *How the Akkadian Empire Was Hung Out to Dry.* Science Mag., Aug. 20, 1993, Vol. 261, pg. 985

Gur, Aviv Rettig, *10,000 Year old house uncovered outside Jerusalem*. The Times of Israel, Nov. 25, 2013.

INTERNET ARTICLES AND SITES

ReligionFacts: http://www.religionfacts.com/judaism/beliefs/afterlife.htm

Judaism 101: http://www.jewfaq.org/olamhaba.htm. Jewish theology on afterlife.

J.Q. Jacobs, Gobekli Tepe: http://jqjacobs.net/blog/gobekli_tepe.html. Article on the 12,000 year old Stonehenge-like temple at Gobekli Tepe in southern Turkey.

Gerard Gertoux, Dating the Chedorlaomer's death. www.academia.edu/2642423. Article on the time of death of the Persian king in *the four kings against five* in Genesis.

Gerard Gertoux, Dating the war of the Hyksos. http://www.academia.edu. Article on the timeline that the Hyksos ruled in the Nile Delta of Egypt.

Jean Nougaryol et al. (1968) Ugartica V: 87-90 no. 24, www.scriba.com/doc/Ugarit. Letter RS 18.147 from Ugaritic literature.

Berger, Wolfgang H., http://www.earthguide.ucsd.edu/climate_change. Syllabus for class at UCSC on Climate Change, 1: The Earth's Climate System.

Heiser, Michael S. PhD, https://www.logos.com/ugaritic. *What's Ugaritic Got to do with anything*? Dr. Heiser's article explains the great help the Ugaritic letters gave to bible scholars in correcting some grammatical errors by Hebrew scribes.

Biblical stories in the Qur'an, Section VI, Nr. 10, *Abraham renounce his father* http://www.answering-islam.org/Index/Stories/abraham.htm

Chart showing the development of cuneiform writing in ancient Sumer. http://pandora.cii.wwu.edu/vajda/ling201/writingsystems/sumerian_cuneiform.htm

Development of Mathematics in ancient Sumer. http://www.storyof
mathematics.com/sumerian.html

USE OF THE INTERNET FOR SOURCES

Dictionary.com: The use of the internet is a way of life in today literary culture. I have used this internet source for quick definition of terms not familiar to our everyday discourse.

Wikipedia (http://en.wikipedia.org/): I have occasionally referred to articles or facts mentioned in Wikipedia. This site is written by anonymous internet volunteers. For this reason there is some question on the use of information from this site in historical papers. However, most of our study is of ancient history which is usually without controversy. Wikipedia has highly footnoted these ancient history articles with source books or sites. I have researched the footnote sources to document the facts in few times I have quoted Wikipedia.

During the research for this book, I have consulted hundreds of websites to find the information necessary for each topic. In many cases, one site will lead to another which will lead to a book or article that I have credited in the footnotes. Sometimes the information from various sources leads to information supplied in this book that is not fully accredited as it becomes difficult to identify the exact source. I have tried to credit any source I have found; but there may be some I have missed. I apologize to any author for this unintended oversight.

INDEX

Printed in the United States
By Bookmasters